ON

CORAL REEFS AND ISLANDS.

BY

JAMES D. DANA,

GEOLOGIST OF THE EXPLORING EXPEDITION AROUND THE WORLD DURING THE YEARS 1838—1842, C. WILKES, U. S. N., COMMANDER.

"We wandered where the dreamy palm
Murmured above the sleeping wave ;
And through the waters clear and calm
Looked down into the coral cave,
Whose echoes never had been stirred
By breath of man or song of bird."

THULIA, J. C. PALMER, U. S. N., EXPL. EXP.

FROM THE AUTHOR'S EXPLORING EXPEDITION REPORT ON GEOLOGY, WITH ADDITIONS.

NEW YORK:
G. P. PUTNAM & Co.
1853.

CONTENTS.

CHAPTER I.

STRUCTURE OF CORAL REEFS AND ISLANDS.

CHAPTER II.

STRUCTURE GROWTH AND HABITS OF CORAL ZOOPHYTES.

CHAPTER III.

FORMATION OF REEFS AND CAUSES OF THEIR FEATURES AND GEOGRAPHICAL DISTRIBUTION.

CHAPTER IV.

CHAPTER V.

ON CHANGES OF LEVEL IN THE PACIFIC OCEAN.

NOTE.—By a recent letter from Rev. C. F. Winslow, we are informed that he has examined with acids the supposed coral material on Maui, referred to on p. 132, and found that it does not effervesce and is not calcareous. It is therefore no evidence of an elevation of the island.

ON

CORAL REEFS AND ISLANDS.

CHAPTER I.

STRUCTURE OF CORAL REEFS AND ISLANDS.

1. General Features of Coral Reefs and Islands.

The general features of coral reefs and islands have often been delineated by travellers, and are probably almost as familiar to the reader as the scenes of the land around us. Yet a few brief remarks on this point form a necessary introduction to the more minute descriptions of structure which follow.

Coral reefs.—A wide platform of rock covered by the sea except at low tide, borders most of the high islands of the Pacific. It is a vast accumulation of coral, based upon the bottom in the shallow waters of the shores. This bank or table of coral rock, is of varying width, from a few hundred feet to a mile or more; and although the surface is usually nearly flat, it is often intersected by irregular boat channels, or occasionally encloses large bays, affording harbor protection to scores of ships. In very many instances the reef stands at a distance from the shores like an artificial mole, leaving a wide and deep channel between it and the land; and within this channel are other coral reefs, some in scattered patches and others attached to the shore. The inner reef in these cases, is distinguished as the *fringing* reef, and the outer as the *barrier* reef. The sea rolls in heavy surges against the outer margin of the barrier; but the still waters of a lake prevail within, affording safe navigation for the tottling canoe sometimes through the whole circuit of an island: and not unfrequently, ships may pass, as by an internal canal, from harbor to harbor around the land. The reef is covered by the sea at high tide, yet the smoother waters indicate its extent, and a line of breakers its outline. Occasionally a green island rises from the reef, and in some instances, a grove of palms stretches along the barrier for miles, where the action of the sea has raised the coral structure above the waves.

The annexed sketch conveys some idea of the peculiar features presented by a Pacific island and its encircling reefs, though in order to fill out the scene, the jagged heights and deep gorges of the island should be covered with forests and the shores with groves and native villages. The coral platform which borders the

shore is represented with its usual uneven line, its broad harbors with a narrow entrance, and to the left, an irregular ship channel running between the inner or fringing reef, and the outer or barrier. At a single place, the sea is faced by a cliff; and here, owing to the boldness of the shores and depth of waters, the reef is wanting. To the right there is only a fringing reef.

Coral islands.—Coral islands resemble the reefs just described, except that a lake or lagoon is encircled instead of a mountainous island. A narrow rim of coral reef, generally but a few hundred yards wide, stretches around the enclosed waters. In some parts the reef is so low that the waves are still dashing over it into the lagoon; in others it is verdant with the rich foliage of the tropics. The coral-made land when highest is seldom more than eight or ten feet above high tide.

When first seen from the deck of a vessel, only a series of dark points is descried just above the horizon. Shortly after, the points enlarge into the plumed tops of cocoa-nut trees, and a line of green, interrupted at intervals, is traced along the water's surface. Approaching still nearer, the lake and its belt of verdure are spread out before the eye, and a scene of more interest can

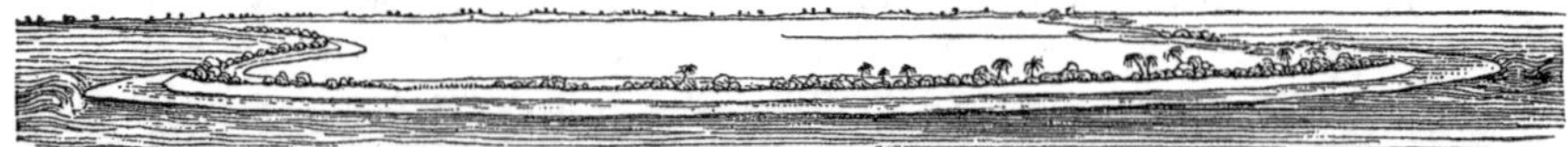

scarcely be imagined. The surf beating loud and heavy along the margin of the reef, presents a strange contrast to the prospect beyond,—the white coral beach, the massy foliage of the grove, and the embosomed lake with its tiny islets. The color of the lagoon water is often as blue as the ocean, although but fifteen or twenty fathoms deep; yet shades of green and yellow are intermingled, where patches of sand or coral-knolls are near the surface; and the green is a delicate apple-shade, quite unlike the ordinary muddy tint of shallow waters.

The belt of verdure, though sometimes continuous around the lagoon, is usually broken into islets separated by varying intervals of bare reef; and through one or more of these intervals, a ship-channel occasionally opens into the lagoon. The larger coral islands are thus a string of islets along a line of reef. The king of the Maldives bears the high-sounding title of "Ibrahim Sultan King of the thirteen Atollons and Twelve Thousand Isles;" which Capt. W. F. W. Owen, R. N., remarks, is no exaggeration.

A few small coral islands are simple reefs without lagoons. In some cases they are bare banks of coral; but generally, the usual vegetation of the islands has obtained a foothold, and affords some protection against the glare of the coral sand.

With these general remarks we may enter upon the more particular consideration of the characters of reefs and islands.

2. Characters of Fringing and Barrier Reefs.

a. General features.—Fringing reefs have been described as those that directly adjoin the shores of an island; and the *barrier*, as the exterior reefs, separated from the fringing reef, or from the shores when there is no inner reef, by an open channel.

While there are only narrow shore-reefs to many islands, around others, a distant barrier extends like an artificial mole, sometimes ten or even fifteen miles from the land, and enclosing not only one, but at times several islands. Between the narrow fringing platform and these remote barriers, there is every possible variation as to extent and relative position. The inner channel is sometimes barely deep enough at low tide for canoes, or for long distances may be wanting entirely. Then again, it is a narrow intricate passage, obstructed by knolls or patches of coral, rendering the navigation dangerous. Again, it is for miles in length an open sea, in which ships find room to beat against a head wind with a depth of twenty, thirty, or even fifty fathoms. Yet hidden reefs make caution necessary. Patches from a few square feet to many square miles in extent are met with over the broad area enclosed by these distant barriers.

These varieties of form and position are well exemplified in a single group of islands—the Feejees; a chart of which Archipelago by the Expedition is inserted at the close of this volume.

Near the middle of the chart is the island *Goro;* its shores, excepting the western, are bordered by a fringing reef. The island *Angau*, south of Goro, is encircled by a coral breakwater, which on the southern and western sides runs far from the shores, and is a proper barrier reef, while on the eastern side, the same reef is attached to the coast and is a fringing reef. From these examples we perceive the close relation of barrier and fringing reefs. While a reef is sometimes quite encircling, in other instances it is interrupted or wholly wanting along certain shores; and occasionally it may be confined to a single point of an island.

Above Angau lies *Nairai;* though a smaller island than Angau the barrier reef is of greater extent, and stretches off far from the shores. To the eastward of Nairai are *Vatu Rera*, *Chichia*, and *Naiau*, other examples of islands fringed around with narrow reefs. *Lakemba*, a little more to the southward, is also encircled with coral: but on the east side the reef is a distant barrier. In *Aiva*, immediately south of Lakemba, the same structure is exemplified; but the coral ring is singularly large for the little spots of land it encloses. The *Argo Reef*, east of Lakemba, is a still larger barrier, encircling two points of rock called Bacon's isles. It is actually a large lagoon island, twenty miles long, with some coral islets in the lagoon, and two of basaltic constitution, of which the largest is only a mile in diameter. Aiva and Lakemba are in fact other lagoon islands, in which the rocky islands of the interior bear a larger proportion to the whole area. The same view is further illustrated by comparing the Argo reef with Nairai, Angau, or Moala: these cases differ only in the greater or less distance of the reef from the shores and the extent of the enclosed land.

Passing to the large islands *Vanua Levu* and *Viti Levu*, we observe the same peculiarities illustrated on a much grander scale. Along the southern shores of Viti Levu, the coral reef lies close against the coast; and the same is seen on the east side and north extremity of Vanua Levu. But on the west side of these islands, this reef stretches far off from the land, and in some parts is even twenty-five miles distant, with a broad sea within. This sea, however, is obstructed by reefs, and along the shores there are proper fringing reefs.

The forms of encircling reefs depend evidently to a great extent on that of the land they enclose. That this is the case even in the Argo reef and such other examples as offer now but a single rock above the surface of the enclosed lagoon, we shall endeavor to make apparent, if not already so, when the cause of the forms of coral islands is under discussion. Yet it is also evident that this correspondence is not exact, for many parts of the shores, and sometimes more than half the coast, may be exposed to the sea, while other portions are protected by a wide barrier.

In recapitulation, we remark, that reefs around islands may be (1) entirely encircling; or they may be (2) confined to a larger or a smaller portion of the coast, either continuous or interrupted: they may (3) constitute throughout a distant barrier; or (4) the reef may be fringing in one part and a barrier in another; or (5) it may be fringing alone: the barrier may be (6) at great distances from the shores, with a wide sea within, or (7) it may so unite to the fringing reef that the channel between will hardly float a canoe. These points are sustained by all reef regions.

A wide difference in the extent of reefs would be inferred from these facts. There is the mere point of coral rock; and again, as for example, west of the two large Feejee islands, there may be three thousand square miles of continuous reef-ground, occupied with coral patches and intermediate channels or seas. The enclosing barrier off Vanua Levu alone is more than one hundred miles long. The Exploring Isles, in the eastern part of the Feejee group, have a barrier eighty miles in circuit. New Caledonia, as often cited, has a reef along its whole western shores, a distance of two hundred and fifty miles, and it extends one hundred and fifty miles farther north, adding this much to the length of the island. The great Australian barrier forms a broken line, a thousand miles in length, lying off the coast from the Northern Cape to the tropical circle; and the channel within is in some parts sixty miles from the coast, with a depth of thirty to sixty fathoms.

The seas outside of the lines of coral reef are often unfathomable within a short distance of the line of breakers.

b. Structure of Reef Formations.

In the description of reef grounds or reef-formations there are several distinct subjects for consideration, as is obvious from the preceding remarks. These are—

1. *Outer reefs*, or reefs formed from the growth of corals exposed to the open seas. Of this character, are all proper barrier reefs, and such fringing reefs as are unprotected by a barrier.

2. *Inner reefs*, or reefs formed in quiet water between a barrier and the shores of an island.

3. *Channels* or *seas within barriers*, which may receive detritus either from the reefs, or the shores, or from both of these sources combined.

4. *Beaches and beach formations*, produced by coral accumulations on the shores through the action of the sea and winds.

The outer and inner reefs, channels, and beaches, act each their part in producing the coral formations in progress about islands.

Outer reefs.—The outer reefs or flats of coral rock receive the waves along their margin; and the outline exposed to this action is very much cut up with deep channels which give passage to the advancing waters, and to the currents that flow back in preparation for the next breaker. This margin, which we have said rises but little above low-tide level, usually slopes beneath the water at an angle of forty to seventy degrees to a depth of three to eight fathoms; thence the waters deepen very gradually for one to five hundred yards out, and from this there is finally an abrupt descent, generally by an angle of at least forty degrees to depths beyond the reach of a sounding lead. There is a great difference in the rapidity with which the water deepens, as might be inferred from the varied character of submarine slopes; in some cases the shallow waters may extend for two or three miles beyond the reef, but it is far more common to meet with the opposite extreme—unfathomable depths within a few hundred feet.

The growing corals are mostly confined to the shallow waters of the reef, and to its sloping margin up which they extend to within a foot or less of the surface. In these shallow waters the various zoophytes at times are crowded over extensive areas; yet very often they occur only in patches scattered throughout large fields of coral debris. The top of the reef is mostly destitute of life, and consists of the naked coral rock, more or less covered with coral sand. Yet there are some shallow pools, especially towards the outer limits, which abound in corals.

The exposed edge of the reef is commonly raised a few inches above the general surface, and is, therefore, the first part laid bare by the retreating tide, although a dangerous place for a ramble, on account of the heavy breakers. Though very uneven, the surface has generally a smooth, water-worn appearance, and is spotted with various shades of pink and purple. These colors, as observed by Chamisso, are due to incrusting Nullipores, that grow like lichens over the rock: they are vegetable in nature, though composed mostly of lime. Other nodular and branching Nullipores, some sprigs of Madrepores, and a few of Astræas grow in the more sheltered cavities, where they are not easily dislodged by the waves; and among them, despite the breakers, cling numerous echini, asterias, and actiniæ. The gradual wear of the reefs by the wash of the sea is prevented, to a great extent, by these Nullipore incrustations, as was pointed out by Darwin.* He states that on Keeling's Island they constitute a layer two or three feet in thickness, with a breadth of twenty feet. They are abundant on the Paumotu reefs.

The outer reefs are distinguished in many parts from the inner by becoming covered with accumulations of coral fragments and sand, which are thrown up by the waves: finding a lodgment some distance back from the margin of the reef, the accumulations gradually increase, till in many instances they form dry land, and prepare the way for vegetation. Such effects are mostly confined, however, to the sides open to the prevailing wind, and are generally of limited extent. Occasionally, as at Bolabola, the reef for miles in length is changed from the submerged coral bank into a habitable islet—a green belt to the island of rocks and forests within. The causes and the result are much the same as in the case of the lagoon island, and the steps in the process will be more particularly described when treating of the coral atoll.

---

* Darwin on Coral Reefs, London, 1842, page 9, and elsewhere.

The rock of the reef, wherever broken, exhibits a compact texture. In some parts it consists of coral fragments of quite large size firmly cemented: other portions are a finer coral breccia, or conglomerate: and still others, more common, are solid white limestones, as impalpable and homogeneous in texture as the secondary limestone of our continents, and usually much harder. It is rare to meet with any corals in this reef-rock retaining the original position of growth. It is at once apparent that the rock consists of the debris of the coral fields, consolidated by a calcareous cement; and the great abundance of the finer variety of rock indicates that much of it has originated from coral sand or mud. Wherever broken, it is found to present the same character as here described, a texture indicating a detritus origin. This reef-rock is formed in the midst of the waves; and we shall hereafter show that to this fact it owes many of its peculiarities. Besides corals, the shells of the seas contribute to it, and it sometimes contains them as fossils, along with bones of fish, exuviæ of crabs, spines and fragments of echini, and other remains of organic life inhabiting reef-grounds.

Inner reefs.—In the still waters of the inner channels or lagoons, when of large extent, we find corals growing in their greatest perfection, and the richest views are presented to the explorer of coral scenery. There are many regions—in the Feejes, examples are common—where a remote barrier encloses as pure a sea as the ocean beyond; and the greatest agitation is only such as the wind may excite on a narrow lake or channel. This condition gives rise to some important peculiarities of structure in the inner reefs.

In the general appearance of the surface, however, they much resemble the outer reefs. They are nearly flat, and though mostly bare of life, and much covered with coral sand, there are seldom any large accumulations of coral debris. The margin is generally less abrupt; yet there is every variety, from the gradually sloping bed of corals to the bluff declivity with its clinging clumps. In different parts, there are many portions still under water at the lowest tides; and here, (as well as upon the outer banks,) fine fishing sport is afforded the natives, who wade out at ebb tide with spears, pronged sticks, and nets, to supply themselves with food. The lover of the marvellous may find abundant gratification by joining in such a ramble; among coral plants and flowers, with fishes of fantastic colors, starfish, echini, and myriads of other beings which science alone has named, fit inhabitants of a coral world, there is on every side occasion for surprise and admiration.

Between the large reefs, which spread a broad surface at the water's edge of lifeless coral rock, sometimes of great extent, there are other patches, still submerged, which are covered with growing corals throughout. They are of different elevations; and though at times but a few yards in breadth, there is often alongside of them a depth of many fathoms. They sometimes seem to grow up from a narrow base, like a mushroom; and a ship striking one with her keel may crush it and glide on. More frequently, they are below like the solid reef above described, and the contest is more likely to be fatal to the vessel than to the coral patch. Corals grow over them, as in the shallow waters about other reefs; and, as elsewhere, there are deep cavities among the congregated corals, in which a lead will sometimes sink to a depth of several feet, or even fathoms. These holes about growing reefs often give much annoyance to the boat which may venture to anchor upon them; and in many an instance in the course of the surveys, diving was the only resource left for freeing the foul anchor.

The rock of the inner reefs is peculiar in being but sparingly fragmentary. The corals composing it stand to a great extent as they grew; yet it is not less compact or firm in its texture than the rock of the outer reefs. The cavities among the branches and growing masses gradually become filled with coral sand, and the whole is finally cemented and thoroughly compacted. At Tongatabu and among the Feejee Islands, reefs thus made of corals standing in their growing positions are common. Though now mere dead rock, the limits of the several constituent coral masses may be distinctly made out. Some individual specimens of Porites in the rock of the inner reef of Tongatabu were twenty-five feet in diameter; and Astræas and Meandrinas, both there and in the Feejees, measured twelve to fifteen feet. These corals, when growing beneath the water, form solid hemispheres, or rounded hillocks; but on reaching the surface, the top dies, and enlargement takes place only on the sides. In this manner the hemisphere is finally changed to a broad cylinder with a flat top. This was the condition of the Astræas and Porites in the reef-rock referred to. The platform looks like a Cyclopean pavement, except that the cementing material, filling in between the huge masses, is more solid than any work of art: it even exceeds in compactness the corals themselves. Other portions of these reefs consist of *branching* corals, with the intervals filled in by sand and small fragments; for even in the more still waters fragments are to some extent produced.* There is also to be found here, and frequently over large areas, the solid white limestone already described, showing internally no evidence of its coral origin, and containing rarely a few shells or imbedded fossils.

The formation of the inner reefs goes on at a less rapid rate than that of the outer, as the process depends on growth unaided, except in a comparatively small degree, by the action of the waves. Moreover, as we shall explain more particularly in another place,

* A rock of this kind is often used for buildings and for walls on the island of Oahu. It consists mainly of Porites, and in many parts is still cavernous, or but imperfectly cemented. It is the material of the large church at Honolulu.

impure or fresh waters and currents often operate to retard their growth.

Owing to the last mentioned cause, the inner reefs are not usually joined close to the beach. They stand off a little, separated by an interval of shallow water. At Mathuata, in the Feejees, however, the reef extends quite up; and it is the more remarkable as the country is a plain, the site of a Feejee village, and a mile or two back stands a high bluff. On an island off this part of Vanua Lebu is another example of this fact, and many more might be cited. In such cases, however, there is evidence that the shores upon which the corals grew were bare rocks, instead of moving beach-sands.

From these descriptions it appears that the main distinction between the inner and outer reefs consists in the less fragmentary character of the rock in the former case, the less frequent accumulations of debris on their upper surface, and the more varied features and slopes of the margin. Moreover, the Nullipores, which seem to flourish best in the breakers, are of less extent, or but sparingly met with elsewhere.

The inner margin of a barrier reef, it should be observed, is entitled to rank with inner reefs, as its corals grow in the same quiet waters, and under like circumstances. The variety of coral zoophytes is also greater in the stiller waters, and there are species peculiar to the different regions, as explained in another plaee.

Channels among reefs.—To complete this review of the general appearance and constitution of reef formations, it remains to add some particulars respecting the channels which intervene between coral patches, or separate them from the shores of an island, and also to describe the coral accumulations forming beaches.

The reef of New Holland has been instanced as affording an example of one of the larger reef-channels, varying from thirty to sixty miles in width, and as many fathoms in depth. The reefs west of the large Feejee Islands offer another remarkable example, the reef-grounds being in some parts twenty-five miles wide, and the waters within the barrier, where sounded, twelve to forty fathoms in depth. The barrier in this instance may be from a few hundred yards to a half a mile in width; and some of the inner patches are of the same extent; but by far the larger part of the reef-ground is covered with deep waters, mostly blue like the ocean, and as clear and pure. The sloop of war Peacock sailed along the west coast of both Viti Lebu and Vanua Lebu, within the inner reefs, a distance exceeding two hundred miles. The island of Tahiti on its northern side presents us with a good illustration of a narrow channel, and at the same time exhibits the usual broken or interrupted character of reefs. This is seen in the following cut in which the reefs, both fringing and barrier, are the parts enclosed by dotted lines. The outer reef extends half to two-thirds of a mile from the shore. Within it, between Papieti and Matavai, there is an irregular ship channel, varying from three to twenty fathoms in depth. Occasionally it enlarges into harbors; and in other parts it is very intricate, though throughout navigable by large vessels. The island of Upolu, of the Samoan Group, is bordered by a reef nearly a mile wide on part of its northern shore; but the waters within are too shallow for a canoe at low tide; and therefore, notwithstanding its extent, the reef is rather a fringing than a barrier reef.

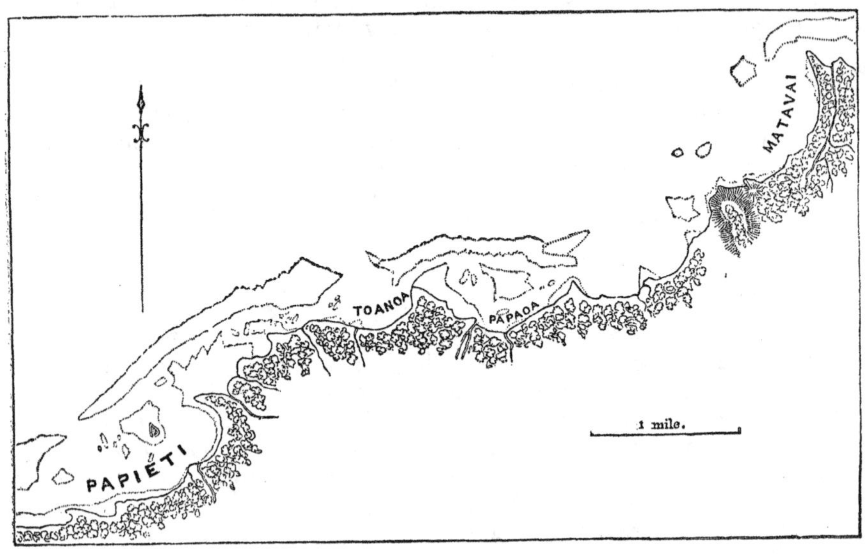

PART OF THE NORTH SHORE OF TAHITI.

The bottom of the channels or lagoons takes its character, as regards the material constituting it, either from the reefs, a source of calcareous sand and fragments, or from the earthy detritus of the island streams. At Upolu, the white coral sand of the reefs, (or in more general terms the reef debris,) forms the bottom; in some places it had the consistence of mud, and it was seldom observed to be covered with coarse material. There were some small patches of coral over it, and here and there a growing mass of Porites. The fresh waters of the shores do not flow over these wide reefs as there is no proper inner channel, and there is consequently no shore detritus mingled with the reef debris. At Tahiti, the sounding lead usually brought up sand, shells, and fragments of coral. At Tongatabu, the bottom, where the Peacock anchored, was a grayish blue mud, appearing as plastic as common clay; it consisted solely of comminuted coral and shells, with coloring matter probably from vegetable decomposition.

To the west of the larger Feejee islands, soundings commonly indicated a bottom of basaltic mud, and this material was frequently brought up with our dredges. On the north side of Vanua Lebu, a stream has so filled with its detritus the wide channel into which it empties, that for a mile our ship dragged its keel in the mud, although elsewhere the water had been from twelve to twenty fathoms deep; and at least half a dozen square miles of land had been added to the shores from this source. Though due principally to shore material, the reefs have probably added somewhat to these accumulations; yet little coral sand can be detected in the mud by the eye, and the proportion is certainly very small. In many places where we anchored, having the reef not more than five hundred yards from the ship, we might have judged, from the character of the bottom, that there were no corals nor shells within many miles. When the materials from both sources, the shore and the reef, are mingled, the proportion will necessarily depend on the proximity to the mouths of streams, the breadth of the inner waters or channels, and the direction and force of the currents. These tidal currents often have great strength, and are much modified and increased in force at certain places, or diminished in others, by the position of the reef with reference to the land. Sweeping on, they carry off the coral debris from some regions to others distant; and again they bear along only the shore detritus, and distribute it. It is thus seen that the same region may differ widely in its adjacent parts, and seemingly afford evidence in one place that there is no coral near, and in another no basaltic land, although either is within a few rods, or even close along side. The extent of the land in proportion to the reef will have an obvious effect upon the character of the channel or lagoon depositions. When the island stands like Bacon's isles, (Feejees,) as a mere point of rock in a wide sea enclosed by a distant barrier, the streams of the land are small and their detritus quite limited in amount. In such a case, the reef and the growing patches scattered over the lagoon, are the sources of nearly all the material that is accumulated upon the bottom.

Shore accumulations.—The wide coral banks and the enclosed channels greatly enlarge the limits tributary to the islands they encircle. They afford extensive fishing grounds for the natives and internal waters which enable them to practice and improve their skill in navigation, and communicate without danger between distant settlements; and the effect is evident in the spirit of maritime enterprise which characterizes the islanders: for these circumstances have favored the construction of large sail-canoes, in which they venture beyond their own land, and often undertake voyages hundreds of miles in length. Instead of a rock-bound coast, harborless and thinly habitable, like most extra-tropical islands, the shores are blooming to the very edge, and wide plains are spread out with breadfruit and other tropical productions. Ports, safe for scores of vessels, are also opened by the same means, and some islands number a dozen, when the unprotected shores would have hardly offered a single good anchorage. Coral reefs are sometimes viewed as only traps to surprise and wreck the unwary mariner. But one who has visited the dreary prison-house, St. Helena, can have some appreciation of the benefits derived from the growth of the zoophyte.

The area of level shores, alluded to as added to many of the high islands by this means, is one of the most striking of these benefits. These plains are sometimes of large extent. The reefs stop the detritus from the hills, and are thus the means of its being added again to the land: they prevent, therefore, the waste which is constantly going on about islands without such barriers; for the ocean not only encroaches upon the unguarded shores of the smaller islands, but carries off whatever the streams may empty into it. The delta of Rewa, on Viti Lebu, resulting from the detritus accumulations of a large river, covers nearly sixty square miles. This is an extreme case in the Pacific, as few islands are so large, and consequently rivers of such magnitude are not common. But there is rarely an island which has not at least some narrow plains from this source; and upon them the villages of the natives are usually situated. Around Tahiti these plains are from half a mile to two or three miles in width, and the cocoanut and breadfruit groves are mostly confined to them.

Beach sandrock.—Besides the accumulations from a shore source, there are also beach formations derived from the reefs. The tides and the attending currents carry to the shores more or less coral sand with shells and other reef-relics, and these sometimes form large deposits. The material is mostly like common sand in fineness, but often somewhat coarser, or even like a bank of pebbles. When the barrier is distant, only the sand and smaller pebbles are met with; but if the reef is quite narrow, there may be larger fragments and masses of coral rock.

These deposits become cemented by being alternately moistened and dried, through the action of the recurring tides, and the wash of the sea on the shores. The waters take up some carbonate of lime which is deposited and hardens among the particles on the evaporation of the moisture at the retreat of the tides. In some places the grains are loosely coherent, and seem to be united only by the few points in contact; and with a little care, the calcareous coating which caused the union may be distinctly traced out. In other cases, the sand has been changed to an oolite, or to a solid rock, the interstices having been filled till a compact mass was formed. Generally, even the most solid varieties show evidence of a sand origin, and in this they differ from the reef-rock. The pebbly beds produce a pudding-stone of coral.

In all instances observed, these calcareous sand-rocks or conglomerates form a number of parallel layers along the coast, which dip regularly at an angle of five to eight degrees towards the water. The layers are from a few inches to a foot in thickness. They appear as if they had been tilted by some force from below, and are seen to outcrop successively, on receding from the water. Tutuila and Upolu in the Navigator Group, and Oahu in the Hawaiian, afforded us many examples of these beach formations. They seldom rise more than a few inches above high tide. At certain localities they appear to have been washed away after they were formed; and occasionally large masses or slabs have been uplifted by the sea, and thrown back on the beach.

Deposits of the same kind sometimes included detritus from the hills. Black basaltic pebbles are thus cemented by the white calcareous material, producing a rock of very singular appearance. Near Diamond Hill on Oahu, is a good locality for observing the steps in its formation. Many of the pebbles of the beach are covered with a thin incrustation of carbonate of lime, appearing as if they had been dipped in milk, and others are actually cemented, yet so weakly that the fingers easily break them apart.

The lime in solution in waters washing over these coral shores, is also at times deposited in the cavities or seams of the basaltic rocks; the cavities of the lava or basalt become filled with white calcareous kernels, and the cellular lava is changed into an amygdaloid. In large cavities or caverns, it often forms stalactites or stalagmitic incrustations.*

Drift sand-rock.—Still another kind of beach formation is going on in some regions through the agency of the winds in connection with the sea. It occurs only on the windward side of islands when the reefs are narrow, and proceeds from the drift sands.

The drifts resemble ordinary sand-drifts, and are often quite extensive. On Oahu, they occur at intervals around the eastern shores, from the *northern* cape, to Diamond Point which forms the *south* cape of the island,—the part exposed to the trades; and they are in some places twenty to forty feet in height. They are most remarkable on the north cape, a prominent point exposed to the winds that blow occasionally from the westward, as well as to the regular trades. They also occur on Kauai, another of the Hawaiian Islands. But at Upolu, (Samoa,) where the protecting reefs are broad, I met with no instance worthy of mention.

These sand-banks, through the agency of infiltrating waters, fresh or salt, become cemented into a sand-rock, more or less fri-

* Similar facts are stated by Mr. Darwin as observed on the shores of Ascension, and many interesting particulars are given respecting calcareous incrustations on coasts.—See Volc. Islands, p. 49. They were observed by the writer upon Madeira, in St. Jago, one of the Cape Verds, as well as among the basaltic islands of the Pacific.

able. The rock consists of thin layers or laminæ, which are very distinct, and indicate, generally, every successive drift of sand which puffs of wind had added in the course of its formation: and where a heavier gale had blown off the top of a drift, and new accumulations again completed it, the whole history is distinctly displayed in the rock. Several catastrophes of this kind may be made out from the character of the lamination in the sand-bluffs on the north side of Oahu. Since their formation, this island has undergone an elevation of twenty-five or thirty feet; these hills, once on the shores, are now seventy feet above the level of the sea, and they face the water with a bluff front (due to degradation), in which the lamination is finely exposed to view. The structure is best seen in a transverse section, presented on the west side. The layers are but a fraction of an inch thick: at one of the hills large slate-like slabs may be obtained; they have a sanded surface, but are so hard within as to clink under the hammer. A particular description of these bluffs is given in the author's remarks on the geology of the Hawaiian islands.

BLUFFS OF CORAL SAND-ROCK, NORTH SHORE OF OAHU.

One of the most interesting facts, observed in connection with these drift hills, is the absence of shells, and even of fragments of shells or corals, sufficiently large to be referred to either of these sources. The material is a fine sand, without organic remains, although situated on shores off which, within a hundred yards, there are shells and corals innumerable.

c. Thickness of reefs.

We have considered in the preceding pages the peculiarities of form and structure characterizing the reef formations bordering islands and continents, and their influence upon the enclosed land. Could we raise one of these coral-bound islands from the waves, we should find that the reefs stand upon the submarine slopes, like massy structures of artificial masonry; some forming a broad flat platform or shelf ranging around the land, and others encircling it like vast ramparts, perhaps a hundred miles or more in circuit. The reefs that were near the water-line of the coast would be seen to have stood in the shallowest water, while the outer ramparts rested on the more deeply submerged slopes. Indeed, it is obvious that with a given slope to the declivity of the land, the thickness of the reef resting upon it may be directly determined, as it would be twice as great two hundred feet from the shore as at one hundred feet. The only difficulty, therefore, in correctly determining the depth or thickness of any given reef, arises from the uncertainty with regard to the submarine slope of the land. It is, however, admitted as the result of extensive observation, that in general these slopes correspond nearly with those of the land above water. Mr. Darwin has thus estimated the thickness of the reefs of the Gambier Group and some other Pacific islands, and he arrives at the conclusion, as his figures indicate, that some coral reefs, at their outer limits, are at least *two thousand feet* in thickness.

It will be shown in another part of this volume, that the mountain slopes of the islands of the Pacific, except when increased by degrading agents, cannot be assumed to exceed twelve or fourteen degrees, and they are often but half this amount. The slopes of Mauna Kea and Mauna Loa, island of Hawaii, do not average over eight degrees. On the north side of Upolu, where the reefs are wide, the inclination is from three to six degrees. Throughout the Pacific, the *steeper* slopes of the mountains are due to agencies which cannot be shown to have affected the submarine slopes, excepting in cases of disruption of islands by forces below.

Assuming *eight* degrees as the mean inclination, we should have for the depth of reef, (or water,) one mile from the shore, 740 feet; or assuming *five* degrees, 460 feet. Adopting the first estimate, the Gambier Group would give for the outer reef a thickness of at least 1750 feet; or with the second, 1150 feet. The island of Tahiti, (taking the north side for data,) would give in the same manner 250 feet by the last estimate, which we judge to be most correct; Upolu, by the same estimate, 440 feet. The deduction for Upolu may be too large: taking three degrees as the inclination, it gives 260 for the thickness at the outer margin. The results are sufficiently accurate to satisfy us of the great thickness of many barrier reefs.

These calculations, however, are liable to error from many sources. Very different results might generally be obtained from different sides of the same island; and the same group often contains islands without reefs, and others with reefs one or even several miles from the shores. But since we may show that the absence of a reef or its limited extent may be traced to some causes restricting or modifying its formation, it is obvious that the error would probably be on the side of too low an estimate. Adjacent to the larger islands, such as those of Vanua Levu and New Holland, the error might be of the opposite kind; for the slopes of the land are of a more complex or irregular character than on the smaller islands. In the latter, they may be shown to belong generally to a single elevation of igneous origin, or at the most to two or three combined; while in the former, they may pertain to different ranges of hills or mountains. For correct results in any instance, the land and its declivities should be carefully studied beforehand, and the system in its inclinations determined by observation. With regard to Tahiti and Upolu, information bearing upon this point was obtained, and the above conclusions may be received with much confidence. Many of the Feejee reefs, on the same principle, cannot be less than 2000 feet in thickness.

Such accumulations of calcareous rock may appear to be an incredible work for the coral polyp, but only so, because we are not accustomed to contemplate the results which may proceed from the smallest agencies long continued. The operatives in the inorganic world are invisible molecules; and among living organisms, it is the lowest grade, the minims of existence, that have accomplished the grandest results in the earth's history.

3. Coral Islands.

A. Forms and general features of Coral Islands.

A barrier reef, and a lagoon enclosed by it, are the prominent features of a coral island; yet there are a few of small size in which the lagoon is wanting. In the larger islands, the waters within look like the ocean, and are similarly roughened by the wind, though not to the same extent. Standing on the north shore of the Raraka lagoon, (in the Paumotus,) and looking southwest, nothing is descried but blue waters;—far in the distance, to the right or left, a few faint dots are distinguished; and as the eye sweeps around, these gradually enlarge into lines of palms and other verdure, which finally become distinct groves on nearing the observer. At Dean's Island, another of the Paumotus, and at many of the Carolines, the resemblance to the ocean is still more striking. The lagoon is in fact but a fragment of the ocean cut off by more or less perfect walls of coral reef-rock; and the reef is here and there surmounted by verdure, forming a series of islets.

In many of the smaller coral islands, the lagoon has lost its ocean character, and become a shallow lake, and the green islets of the margin have coalesced in some instances into a continuous line of foliage. Traces may perhaps be still detected of the passage or passages over which the sea once communicated with the internal waters, though mostly concealed by the trees and shrubbery which have spread around and completed the belt of verdure. The coral island is now in its most finished state: the lake rests quietly in its bed of palms, hardly ruffled by the storms that madden the surrounding ocean.

From the islands with small lagoons, there is every variety in gradation down to those in which there is no trace of a lagoon. These simple banks of coral are the smallest of coral islands.

These remarks, in connection with the general view given on a preceding page, will prepare the reader to appreciate the following descriptions of various coral islands, illustrating their forms, actual size, and condition.

A single group of islands, the Tarawan or Kingsmills, (see Plate,) affords good examples of the principal varieties. The irregularity of shape and size is at once apparent to the eye. In the southernmost, *Taputeouea*, the form is very narrow, the length being thirty-three miles, with the width of the southern portion scarcely exceeding six miles, and that of the northern more than one-half less. The emerged land is confined to one side, and consists of a series of islets upon the eastern line of coral reef. The western side is for the most part some feet under water, and there is hardly a proper lagoon. Sailing by the island, to windward, the patches of verdure thus strung together seem to rise out of a long white line of breakers, the sea surging violently against the unseen coral reef upon which they rest.

Namouti, the next island north, is about twenty miles long by eight broad. The rim of land, though in fewer islets, is similar to that of Taputeouea in being confind to the reef fronting northeast. The reef of the opposite side, though bare of vegetation, stands near low tide level, and the whole encloses a large lagoon.

Nanouki and *Apamama*, though smaller than Namouti, have the same general character. Nanouki is triangular in shape, and has an islet on the western point or cape, which is quite prominent. Apamama differs from either of the preceding in having two narrow ship entrances to the lagoon, one through the northwestern reef, and another through the southwestern.

---

* The plate is a reduced copy of the chart of these islands, as surveyed by the Exploring Expedition.

Kuria is a remarkable double island, without a proper lagoon. It consists of two neighboring groves, each about a square mile in extent, on adjacent patches of reef.

Maiana is quite regularly quadrangular, with an uninterrupted range of land on two of the four sides, and an exposed reef constituting the other two.

Tarawa consists of two sides of a triangle. The western reef is wanting, and the sea and lagoon have unbroken communication. In place of it, there are two to ten fathoms water, and a bottom of coral sand. Small vessels may sail in almost anywhere on this side to a good anchorage, and there is a passage for ships of the largest size. The depth within is greater than on the bar, and these inner waters obviously correspond to the lagoon of other islands.

Apia has much resemblance to Apamama in its forest border and lagoon. Moreover, there is a ship-entrance through the southwestern reef.

Maraki is one of the prettiest coral islands of the Pacific. The line of vegetation is unbroken; and from the mast-head it lies like a garland thrown upon the waters. The unpracticed eye scarcely perceives, in such a view, the variation from a circular form, however great it may be. The grove is partially interrupted at one point, where there are indications of a former passage through the reef.

Tari-tari is a large triangular atoll. It is wooded almost continuously on the reef facing southeast, and has a few spots of verdure on the southwest, with three entrances to the extensive lagoon. The northern side is a naked reef throughout, scarcely apparent from a ship's deck, except by the long line of breakers. *Makin*, just north of Tari-tari, is a mere patch of coral reef without a lagoon.

We add a few more descriptions of Pacific islands, with figures reduced from the maps of the Expedition to a scale of four tenths of an inch to a mile.

1.

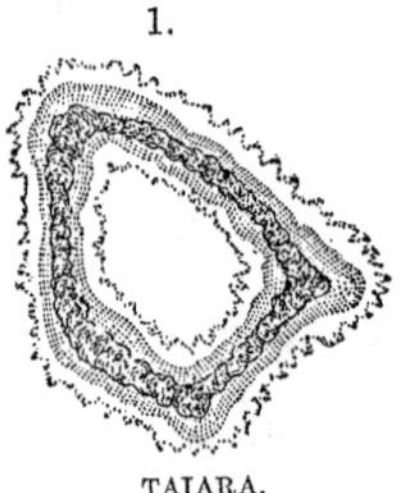

TAIARA.

2.

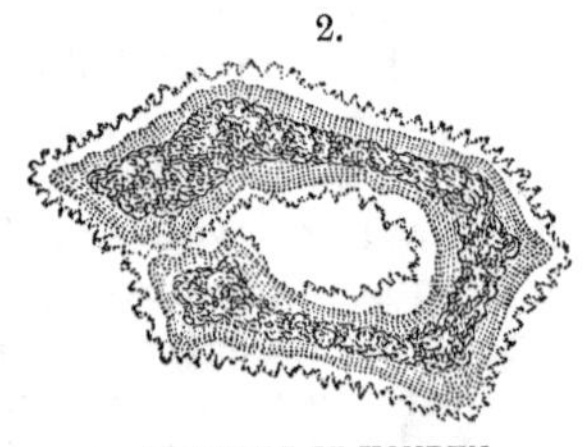

HENUAKE OR HONDEN.

Taiara and *Henuake*, (figs. 1 and 2,) are two small belts of foliage, somewhat similar to Maraki. Henuake possessed an additional charm in being tenanted only by birds; and they were so tame that we took them from the trees as if they had been their flowers.

Swain's and *Jarvis* Islands, (figs. 3 and 4,) are of still smaller size, and have no lagoon. The former is densely covered with foliage, while the surface of the latter is sandy. Swain's Island is a little depressed about the centre, a fact indicating that there was formerly a lagoon.

3.

SWAIN'S ISLAND.

4.

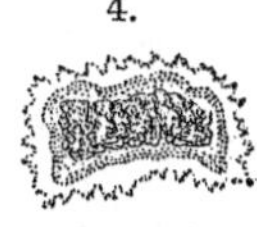

JARVIS ISLAND.

Fakaafo, or Bowditch, (fig. 5,) 200 miles north of Samoa, is the type of a large part of coral islands. The bank of reef has only here and there emerged from the waves and become verdant; in other portions the reef is of the usual height,—that is, near low tide level,—excepting a few spots elevated a little by the accumulation of sand.

5.

FAKAAFO.

The Paumotu Archipelago, the crowded cluster of coral islands just northeast of Tahiti, is a most instructive study for the reader; and a map of these islands by the Expedition, inserted in the Narrative of the Expedition, and also in the Hydrographical Atlas, will well repay close examination. Sailing among these islands—over eighty in number, only four of which are over twelve feet high exclusive of the vegetation,—two or three are almost constantly in sight from the mast-head.

The small amount of habitable land on these reef-islands is one of their most peculiar features. Nearly the whole surface is water; and the land around the lagoon is but a narrow rim, the greater part of which is usually under water at high tide. This fact will be rendered more apparent from the following table, containing a statement of the sizes and areas of several islands, with the amount of habitable land. The measures are given in geographical miles.

	Length.	Greatest breadth.	Area in square miles.	Habitable parts in square miles.
Carlshoff, Paumotus,	27	13	200	10
Wolchonsky, "	15	3	40	3
Raraka, "	15	10	90	8
Manhii, "	14	6½	50	9
Nairsa or Deans, "	50	19	1000	16
Fakaafo, Union Group,	7½	4½	20	2½
Clarence, "	8½	5½	27	2
Taputeouea, Kingsmills,	33	6	60	6
Tarawa, "	20	10	130	8
Namouti, "	22	9	125	7
Tari-tari, "	18	11	110	4

The ten islands here enumerated have an aggregate area of 1952 square miles, while the amount of actual dry habitable land is but seventy-six miles, or less than one twenty-fourth. In the Caroline Archipelago the proportion of land is still smaller. Menchikoff atoll covers an area of 500 square miles, and includes hardly six square miles of wooded land. In the Marshall Islands the dry land is not over one-hundredth of the whole surface; while in the Pescadores the proportion of land to the whole area is about as 1 to 200.

The distribution of the land upon the reef is obvious from the sketches already given. It was long since remarked that the windward side was in general the highest. It is also apparent that there are not only great irregularities of form, but the reef may at times be wholly wanting or deeply submerged on one side.

In many islands there is a ship entrance, sometimes six or eight fathoms deep, through the reef to the lagoons, where good anchorage may be had; but the larger part have only shallow passages, or none at all. In the Paumotus, out of the twenty-eight visited by the Expedition, not one half were found to have navigable entrances. In the Carolines, where the islands are large and not so much wooded, entrances are of more common occurrence. About half of the Kingsmill Islands afford a good entrance and safe anchorage. Through these openings in the reefs, there is usually a rapid outward current, especially during the ebbing tide. At Depeyster Island, it was found to run at the rate of two and a half miles an hour. It was as rapid at Raraka, in the Paumotus, and as Capt. Wilkes remarks, it was difficult to pull a boat against it, into the lagoon.

Soundings about Coral Islands.—The water around coral islands deepens as rapidly and in much the same way as off the reefs about high islands. The atoll usually seems to stand as if stilted up in a fathomless sea. The soundings of the Expedition afford some interesting results.

Seven miles east of Clermont Tonnerre, the lead ran out to 1145 fathoms (6870 feet), without reaching bottom. Within three quarters of a mile of the southern point of this island, the lead, at another throw, after running out for a while, brought up an instant at 350 fathoms, and then dropped off again and descended to 600 fathoms without reaching bottom. On the lead, which appeared bruised, a small piece of white coral was found, and another of red; but no evidence of *living* zoophytes. On the east side of the island, three hundred feet from the reef, a bottom of coral sand was found in 90 fathoms; at one hundred and eighty feet, the same kind of bottom in 85 fathoms; at one hundred and thirty feet, a coral bottom in 7 fathoms;—and from this it decreased irregularly to the edge of the shore reef.

Off the southeast side of Ahii (another of the Paumotus), about a cable's length from the shore, the lead after descending 150 fathoms, struck a ledge of rock, and then fell off and finally brought up at a depth of 300 fathoms.

Two miles east of Serle's Island, no bottom was found at 600 fathoms.

A mile and a half south of the larger Disappointment Island, there was no bottom at 550 fathoms.

Near the eastern end of Metia, no bottom was found with a line of 150 fathoms; and a mile distant, no bottom was reached at 600 fathoms.* In general, for one to five hundred yards from the margin of the shore reef, the water slowly deepens, and then there is an abrupt descent, at an angle of 40 or 50 degrees. The results of earlier voyagers, among whom Beechey stands pre-eminent, correspond with this statement. At considerable depths, as would appear from the above facts, the sides of the coral structure may be vertical or even may overhang the bottom below.

There are examples also of less abrupt slopes. Northwest of the Hawaiian Group, Lisiansky, at the island bearing his name, found shallow water for a distance of six or seven miles; the water deepened to ten or eleven fathoms the first mile, fifteen the second, and at the last throw of the lead there were still but twenty-five fathoms.† Christmas Island affords on its western side another example of gradually deepening waters. Yet these shallow waters terminate finally in a rapid declivity of forty or fifty degrees. Off the prominent angles of an atoll, soundings generally continue much beyond the distance elsewhere, as was first observed by Beechey. At Washington Island, mostly abrupt in its shores, there is a bank, according to the surveys of the Expedition, extending from the east point to a distance of half a mile, and another on the west extending to a distance of nearly two

---

* Beechey, whose observations on soundings are the fullest hitherto published, states many facts of great interest. At Carysfort Island, he found the depth 60 yards from the surf line, 5 fathoms;—80 yards, 13 fathoms;—120 yards, 18 fathoms;—200 yards, 24 fathoms;—and immediately beyond, no bottom with 35 fathoms. At Henderson's Island, soundings continued out 250 yards, where the depth was 25 fathoms, and then terminated abruptly. Off Whitsunday, 500 feet out there was no bottom at 1500 feet.

Darwin states many facts bearing upon this subject, of which we may cite the following.—At Heawandoo Pholo (one of the Maldives) Lieutenant Powell found 50 or 60 fathoms close to the edge of the reef. One hundred fathoms from the mouth of the lagoon of Diego Garcia, Captain Moresby found no bottom with 150 fathoms. At Egmont Island, 50 fathoms from the reef, soundings were struck in 150 fathoms. At Cardoo Atoll, only 60 yards from the reef, no bottom was obtained with a line of 200 fathoms. Off Keeling Island, 2200 yards from the breakers, Captain Fitzroy found no bottom at 1200 fathoms. Mr. Darwin also states that at a depth between five and six hundred fathoms, the line was partly cut as if it had rubbed against a projecting ledge of rock; and deduces from the fact "the probable existence of submarine cliffs."

† Voyage round the world, in the years 1803–6, in the ship Neva, by N. Lisiansky, Captain in the Russian Navy, 4to, London: pp. 254-257.

miles. At Kuria, one of the Kingsmills, soundings continue for three miles from the north extremity, along a bank stretching off from this point to the north-northwest. Many other instances might be cited, but they are seldom as remarkable; yet nearly all islands, especially if the points are much prominent, afford similar facts. It has been said that the reef to leeward is generally less abrupt than that to windward, but no facts were obtained by the Expedition sufficiently definite or extensive to settle this question. It is probably true, yet the difference if any must be slight.

B. Structure of Coral Islands.

The descriptions of reefs and their islets apply with equal force to coral islands. By transferring here the statements respecting the former, we should have a nearly complete account of the latter. The same causes, with scarcely an exception, are at work:—the growing of coral-zoophytes, the action of the waves, oceanic currents, and the winds. This resemblance will be rendered more apparent by a review of their characters; the description will be found to be a simple recapitulation of a former paragraph.

The reef of the coral atoll, as it lies at the surface still uncovered with vegetation, is a platform of coral rock, usually two to four hundred yards wide, and situated so low as to be swept by the waves at high tide. The outer edge, directly exposed to the surf, is generally broken into channels and jagged indentations, along which the waters of the resurging wave drive with great force. Though in the midst of the breakers, the edge stands a few inches, and sometimes a foot, above other parts of the platform; the incrusting *Nullipores* cover it with varied tints, and afford protection from the abrading action of the waves. There are usually three to five fathoms water near the margin; and below, over the bottom which gradually deepens outward, beds of corals are growing profusely among lifeless patches of coral sand and fragments. Often the dead areas much exceed those flourishing with zoophytes, and not unfrequently the clusters are scattered like tufts of vegetation in a sandy plain. The growing corals extend up the sloping edge of the reef, nearly to low tide level. For ten to twenty yards from the margin, the reef is usually very cavernous or pierced with holes or sinuous recesses, a hiding-place for various crabs, or a retreat for the echini, asterias, the sea-anemones, and many a pretty mollusc; and over this portion, the gigantic Chama or Tridacna is generally found lying more than half buried in the solid rock, with barely room to gape a little its ponderous shell, and expose to the waters a gorgeously colored mantle. Farther in are occasional pools and basins, alive with all that lives in these strange coral seas.

The reef-rock, wherever broken, shows a detritus origin. Parts are of compact homogeneous texture, a solid white limestone, without a piece of coral distinguishable, and rarely an imbedded shell. But generally the rock is a breccia or conglomerate, made up of corals cemented into a compact mass, and the fragments of which it consists are sometimes many cubic feet in size.

It is apparent that we are describing a second time an *outer* reef. Without dwelling farther upon its characters, we may pass to the features of the reef when raised above the waters and covered with vegetation.

Sections of coral islands and their lagoons have been given by Captain Beechey and Mr. Darwin. We add another, by way of illustration, although little may be presented that is novel after the excellent descriptions of these authors. Sketches of several of these islands, showing the general relation of the rim of land to the reef and the lagoon within, are given in the Plate of the Kingsmill Group. The following sketch represents a section of the rim of land from the sea on one side, (the left,) to the lagoon on the other. In the view, the part *m a*, represents the shallow sea bordering an island, and abruptly deepening one to six hundred feet from the line of breakers. In these shallow waters are the growing corals; yet, as before stated, a large part is barren sand or coral rock.

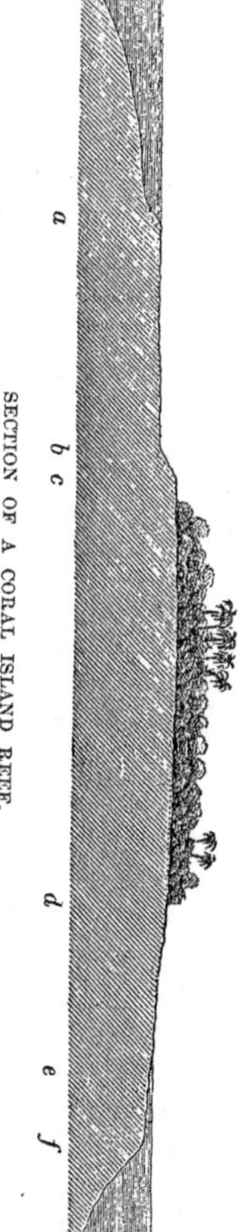

SECTION OF A CORAL ISLAND REEF.

From *a* to *b* is the shore platform of reef-rock, nearly at low tide level, with the margin (*a*) slightly elevated, and much incrusted at the top with Nullipores. From the platform there is a rise by a steep beach (*b c*,) of six or eight feet, to the wooded part of the coral belt represented between *c* and *d*. From *d* to *e* there is a gently sloping beach bordering the lagoon. Beyond *e*, the waters of the lagoon at first deepen gradually, and then fall off more or less abruptly.

In the Paumotus, the shore platform, the steep beach, and the more gently sloping shore of the lagoon are almost constant characteristics.

The width of the whole rim of land, when the island gives no evidence of late elevation, varies from three hundred yards to one-third of a mile, excepting certain prominent points, more exposed to the united action of winds and waves and from opposite directions, which occasionally exceed half a mile.*

* Beechey states that the rim is generally three to four hundred yards in width, and never exceeds half a mile.—*Voyage*, Amer. ed., p. 160.

Shore platform and emerged land.—The shore platform is from one to three hundred feet in width, and has the general features of a half-submerged outer reef. Its peculiarities arise solely from the accumulations which have changed the reef into an island. Much of it is commonly bare at low tide, though there are places where it is always covered with a few inches or a foot of water; and the elevated edge, the only part exposed, often seems like an embankment preventing the water from running off. The tides, as they rise, cover it with water throughout, and bear over it coral fragments and sand, comminuted shells and other animal remains, to add them to the beach. The heavier seas transport larger fragments; and at the foot of the beach there is often a deposit of blocks of coral or coral rock, a cubic foot or so in size, which low tide commonly leaves standing in a few inches of water.†

Besides the deep channels cutting into the margin of the reef and giving it a broken outline, there are in some instances long fissures intersecting its surface. On Aratica, (Carlshoff,) and Ahii, (Peacock Island,) they extended along for a fourth to half a mile, generally running nearly parallel with the shore, and at top were from a fourth to half an inch wide. These fissures are not essential features of the reef, and will come up for consideration on a future page of this work.

The *beach* usually slopes at an angle of 35 to 45 degrees, and consists of coral pebbles or sand, with some worn shells, and occasionally the exuviæ of crabs and bones of fishes. Owing to its whiteness, and the contrast it affords to the massy verdure above, it is a remarkable feature in the distant view of these islands, and often seemed like an artificial wall or embankment running parallel with the shores. On Clermont Tonnerre, the first of these islands visited by us, the natives seen from shipboard, standing spear in hand along the top of the beach, were believed by some to be keeping patrol on the ramparts of a kind of fortification. This deception arose from the dazzling whiteness of the coral sand, in consequence of which, the slope of the beach was not distinguished in so distant a view.

The *emerged land* beyond the beach, in its earliest stage when barely raised above the tides, appears like a vast field of ruins. Angular masses of coral rock, varying in dimensions from one to a hundred cubic feet, lie piled together in the utmost confusion; and they are so blackened by exposure, or from incrusting lich-

† On moving these masses, which generally rest on their projecting angles and have an open space beneath, the waters at once become alive with fish, shrimps, and crabs, escaping from their disturbed shelter; and beneath, appear various Actinæ or living flowers, the spiny echini and sluggish biche-la-mar, while swarms of shells having a soldier crab for their tenant walk off with unusual life and stateliness. Moreover, delicate corallines, Ascidiæ and sponges tint with lively shades of red, green, and pink, the under surface of the block of coral which had formed the roof of the little grotto.

ens, as to resemble the clinkers of Mauna Loa; moreover, they ring like metal under the hammer. Such regions may be travelled over by leaping along from block to block, with the risk of falling into the many recesses among the huge masses. On breaking an edge from the black masses, the usual white color of coral is at once apparent. Some of the blocks, measuring five or six feet in each of their dimensions, were found to be portions of individual corals, while others have the usual conglomerate character of the reef-rock.

In the next stage, coral sand has found lodgment among the blocks; and though so scantily supplied as hardly to be detected without close attention, some seeds have taken root, and vines, purslane, and a few shrubs begin to grow, relieving the scene, by their green leaves, of much of its desolate aspect.

Both of these stages are illustrated on the greater part of coral islands.

In the last stage, the island stands six to ten feet out of water. The surface consists of coral sand, more or less discolored by vegetable or animal decomposition. There is but little depth of coral soil, although the land may appear buried in the richest foliage: and scattered among the trees, stand, still uncovered, many of the larger blocks of coral, with their usual rough angular features and blackened surface. The soil is seldom discolored beyond four or five inches, and but little of it to this depth; there is no proper vegetable mould, but a simple mixture of darker particles with the white grains of coral sand. It is often rather a coral gravel, and below a foot or two, it is usually cemented together into a more or less compact coral rock.

One singular feature of the shore platform, occasionally observed, remains to be mentioned. Huge masses of reef-rock are sometimes found upon it, some of which lie loose upon the reef, while others are firmly imbedded in it below, and so cemented to it as to appear to be actually a part of the platform rock. Sketches of some of these masses are here given.

1.

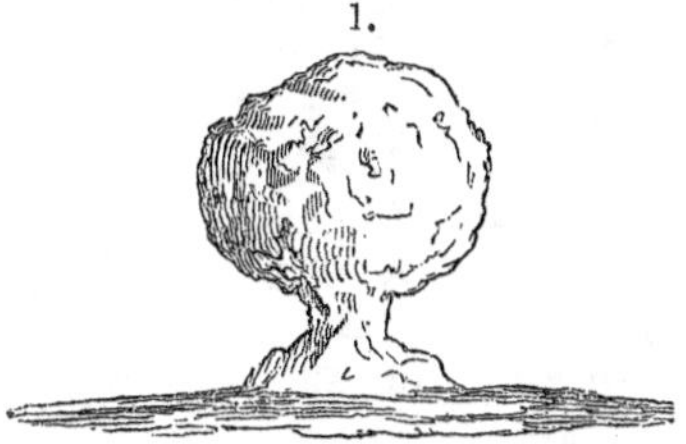

2.

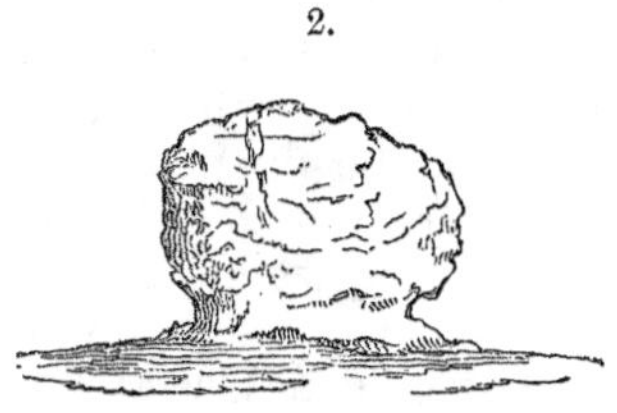

Figure 1 represents a mass on the island of Waterland, (one of the Paumotus,) six feet high, and about five in diameter; it was solid with the reef-rock below, as though a part of it, and about two feet above its base, it had been so nearly worn off by the waters as to have become irregularly top-shape. Figure 2 is another mass, similarly attached to the reef at base, observed on Kawehe, (Vincennes Island.) It was six feet high above low water level, and seven feet in its longest diameter. Below, it had been worn like the one just described, though to a less extent. Another similar mass was eight feet high. Figure 3 represents a block six feet high and ten feet in its longest diameter, seen on Waterland; it was unattached below, and lay with one end raised on a smaller block. On Aratica, (Carlshoff,) others were observed. One loose mass like the last was eight feet high and fifteen feet in diameter, and contained at least a *thousand cubic feet.* Raraka also afforded examples of these attached and unattached blocks, some standing with their tops six feet above high-water mark.

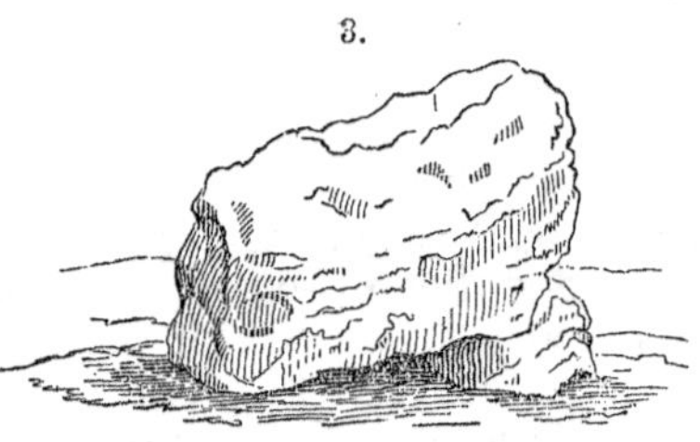
3.

These masses are similar in character to many met with among the fields of blocks just described, and differ only in having been left on the platform instead of being transported over it. Some of them are near the margin of the reef, while others are quite at its inner limit. The third mass figured above was a solid conglomerate, consisting of large fragments of Astræas and Madrepores, and contained some imbedded shells, among which an Ostræa and a Cypræa were noticed. This is their usual character. The other two were parts of large individual corals, (Porites;) but there was evidence in the direction of the cells that they did not stand as they grew; on the contrary, they had been upthrown, and were afterwards cemented with the material of the rock beneath them, probably at the time this rock itself was consolidated. Below some of the loose masses like figure 3, (as on Aratica,) the platform was at times six inches higher than on either side of the mass, owing to the protection from wear given to the surface beneath it. These blocks are always extremely rough and uneven, like those of the emerging land beyond; and the angular features are partly owing in both cases to solution from rains or from the sea-water that may be dashed over them.

It should be distinctly understood that these masses here described were found isolated, and only at considerable intervals. In no instance were they observed clustered. The loose blocks and those cemented below had the same general character, and must have been placed where they were by the same cause, though it may have been at different periods.

The shore of the lagoon is generally low and gently inclined, yet in the larger islands, in which the waters of the lagoon are much disturbed by the winds, there is usually a beach resembling that on the seaward side, though of less extent. A platform of reef-rock at the same elevation as the shore platform sometimes extends out into the lagoon; but it is more common to find it a little submerged and covered for the most part with growing corals: and in either case, the bank terminates outward in an abrupt descent of a few yards or fathoms, to a lower area of growing corals, or a bottom of sand. Still more commonly, we meet with a sandy bottom gradually deepening from the shores without growing coral. These three varieties of condition are generally found in the same lagoon, characterizing its different parts. The lower area of growing corals slopes outward, and usually ceases where the depth is 10 to 12 fathoms; from this there is another descent to the depth which prevails over the lagoon.

On some small lagoons the shore is a thick plastic mud, either white or like clay, and forms a low flat which is very gently sloping. On Henuake, these mud deposits are quite extensive, and of a white color. At Enderby's Island, another having a shallow lagoon, the mud was so deep and thick that there was some difficulty in reaching the waters of the lagoon; the foot sunk in 8 or 10 inches and was not extricated without some difficulty. The color at this island was a dirty brownish clay. This mud is nothing but comminuted coral, so fine as to be almost impalpable.

The *lagoons* of the smaller islands are usually very shallow; and in some, merely a dry bed remains, indicating the former existence of water. Instances of the latter kind are met with only in islands less than three miles in diameter; and those with shallow lagoons are seldom much larger. These shallow waters, when direct communication with the sea is cut off, become, in some instances, very salt by evaporation, and contain no growing coral, with few signs of life of any kind: and in other cases, they are made too fresh for marine life, through the rains. At Enderby's Island the water was not only extremely saline, but the shores of the lagoon were in some places incrusted with salt. But when there is an open channel, or the tides gain access over a bare reef, corals continue to grow, and a considerable portion of the lagoon may be obstructed by them. At Henuake, the sea is shut out except at high water, and there were consequently but few species of corals, and those of small size. At Ahii (Peacock's Island) there was a small entrance to the lagoon, and though comparatively shallow, corals were growing over a large part of it.

In the larger islands, the lagoons contain but small reefs compared with their whole extent; the greater part is an open sea, with deep waters and a sandy bottom. There are instances, as at the southern Maldives, of a depth of 50 and 60 fathoms. Twenty to thirty-five fathoms is the usual depth in the Paumotus. This was the result of Captain Beechey's investigations; and those of the Expedition, though few, correspond. It is however probable that deeper soundings would be found in the large island of Nairsa (Dean's). In the Tarawan Group, south-east of the Carolines, the depth, where examined by the Expedition, varied from 2 to 35 fathoms. Mr. Darwin found the latter depth at Keeling's Island. Chamisso found 25 to 35 fathoms at the Marshall Islands.

The bottom of these large lagoons is very nearly uniform, varying but little except from the occasional abrupt shallowings produced by growing patches of reef. Soundings bring up sand, pebbles, shells, and coral mud; and the last mentioned material appears to be quite common, even in lagoons of considerable size. It has the same character as above described. The bluish clay-like mud of the harbor of Tongatabu may be classed with these deposits.* It appears, therefore, that the finer coral material of the shores prevails throughout the depths of the lagoon. The growing reefs within the lagoons, are in the condition of the *inner* reefs about high islands. The corals grow but little disturbed by the waves, and the reef-rock often contains them in the position of growth. At Taputeouea (Kingsmills or Tarawan Group), reefs very similar to those of the Feejees occur; they present the same large Astræas 10 to 12 feet in diameter, which once were growing where they stand but are now a part of the solid lifeless rock.

Beach formations of coral sandrock are common on the coral islands, and they present the same features in every respect, as those described. They were observed among the Paumotus, on Raraka, Honden, Kawehe, and other islands. The stratified character is always distinct and the layers slope toward the water at the usual small angle, amounting to 5–7 degrees bordering the lagoon, and 7–8 degrees on the seashore side of the land. They often occupy a breadth of 30 to 50 yards, appearing like a series of outcrops; yet not unfrequently they are mostly concealed by the sands of the beach,† and it is probable that they generally underlie the loose surface material of the land. The rock is a fine or coarse sandrock, or a coral pudding-stone, and consists of beach materials. Occasionally it is quite compact, and resembles common limestone, excepting in its whiter color; but generally its sand origin is very apparent.

The *drift sandrock* was not met with by the writer on any coral islands visited, and probably for the reason that opportuni-

* Darwin describes this mud as occurring at the Maldives, and at Keeling Island, (op. cit. p. 26;) Kotzebue mentions it as common at the Marshall Atolls, and Lieutenant Nelson observed it at the Bermudas.

† On the northern atolls of the Maldives, the beach sandrock is said to be quarried out in square blocks and used for building.—*Journ. Geog. Soc.*, v, 400.

ties were not favorable for a thorough exploration. It has been stated that the more exposed points towards the trades, especially the northeast and southwest, are commonly a little higher than other parts; and it is altogether probable that some of the sand heaps, there formed, will prove on examination to afford examples of this variety of coral-rock. Such situations are exactly identical with those on Oahu, where they occur on so remarkable a scale. Mr. R. H. Schomburgh states that on the island of Anegada in the West Indies, the drift banks on the windward shores are forty feet in height.*

Although in these descriptions of atolls, we have dwelt on some points more at length than when describing barrier reefs, still it will be observed that the former have no essential peculiarities of structure apart from such as necessarily arise from the absence of high rocky lands. The encircling atoll-reef, corresponds with the outer reefs that enclose high islands; and the green islets with the beach formations, in the two cases, originate in the same manner.

The lagoons, moreover, are similar in character and position to the inner channels within barrier reefs; they receive only coral material from the action of degrading agents, because no other source of detritus but the reefs is at hand. The accumulations going on within them are, therefore, wholly of coral. The reefs within the lagoons, correspond very exactly in mode of growth and other characters to the *inner* reefs under the lee of a barrier. The corals grow but little disturbed by the waves, and the reef-rock thus formed, often contains them in their natural positions.

The preceding descriptions represent the general character of atolls, but are more especially drawn from the Paumotus. There are some peculiarities in other seas, to which we may briefly allude.

Among the scattered coral islands north of the Samoan Group, the shore platform is seldom as extensive as at the Paumotus. It rarely exceeds fifty yards in width, and is cut up by passages often reaching almost to the beach. It was not unusual for our boats to obtain a landing by watching for a favorable opportunity at the entrance of one of these channels to mount a wave and ride in on its top. In some places the platform is broken into islets. Enderby's Island is one of the number to which this description applies: the beach is eleven or twelve feet high. For the first eight feet, it slopes very regularly at an angle of 30 to 35 degrees, and consists of sand, coarse pebbles, or rounded stones of coral, with some shells; and there is the usual beach conglomerate near the water's edge. After this first slope, it is hori-

* Journal of the Royal Geographical Society, ii, 152. Mr. Schomburgh describes the sandhills as 40 feet in height, and behind the first range, a second, and even a third.

zontal for eighty to two hundred feet, and then there is a gradual rise of three to four feet. Over this portion there are large slabs of the beach conglomerate, along with masses from the reef-rock, and some thick plates of a huge foliaceous Madrepora; and these slabs, many of which are six feet square, lie inclining quite regularly against one another, as if they had been taken up and laid there by hand. They incline in the same direction with the slope of the beach. The large Madrepora alluded to has the mode of growth of the Madrepora palmata; and probably the entire zoophyte extended over an area twelve or fifteen feet in diameter. The fragments are three to four inches thick, and thirty square feet in surface.

As a key to the explanation of the peculiarities here observed, it may be remarked that the tides in the Paumotus are two to three feet, and about Enderby's Island five to six feet in height.

Maldives.—Chagos Bank.—The Maldives have been often appealed to in illustration of coral structures. They are particularly described by Mr. Darwin, from information communicated to him by Captain Moresby, and from the charts of this officer and Lieutenant Powell.* The point of special interest in their structure is the occurrence of atolls or rings within the larger atolls. The islets of the lagoon, and those of the encircling reef, are in many instances annular reefs, each with its own little lake. Gems within gems are here clustered together.

The annular islets of the main encircling reef are oblong, and lie with the longest diameter, which is sometimes three miles long, in the line of the reef. Those of the lagoon are generally less than two miles across. The lagoons they contain vary from five fathoms or less to twelve fathoms in depth.

The Maldives are among the largest atoll-reefs known; and they are intersected by many large open channels; and Mr. Darwin observes, that the interior atolls occur only near these channels, where the sea has free access. We may view each large island in the archipelago as a sub-archipelago of itself. Although thus singular in their features, they illustrate no new principles with regard to reef-formations.†

---

* Darwin on Coral Reefs, p. 32. See also Journal of the Royal Geographical Society, on the Geography of the Maldives, by J. J. Horsburgh, ii, p. 72; and by Captain W. F. W. Owen, ibid, p. 81; also vol. v, p. 398, on the Northern Atolls of the Maldives, by Captain Moresby.

† Mr. Darwin thus remarks, (Op. cit. pp. 33, 34,)—"I can in fact point out no essential difference between these little ring-formed reefs, (which, however, are larger, and contain deeper lagoons than many true atolls that stand in the open sea,) and the most perfectly characterized atolls, excepting that the ring-formed reefs are based on a shallow foundation instead of the floor of the open sea, and that instead of being scattered irregularly, they are grouped closely together."—"It appears from the charts on a large scale, that the ring-like structure is contingent on the marginal channels or branches being wide, and consequently on the whole interior of the atoll being freely exposed to the waters of the open sea. When the

The *Chagos Bank* lies about ten degrees south of the Maldives, and is ninety miles long and seventy broad. The rim is mostly submerged from five to ten fathoms.

Mr. Darwin confirms the opinion of Captain Moresby, that this bank has the character of a lagoon reef, resembling one of the Maldives; and he states on the evidence of extensive soundings, that, if raised to the surface, it would actually become a coral island, with a lagoon forty fathoms deep. In the words of Capt. Moresby, it is in truth nothing more than a half-drowned atoll.*

Metia and other elevated Coral Islands.—In the Chagos Group we have an example of a *sunken* coral atoll. Metia affords an instance of one that has been *elevated* by some force; and several such are met with in the Pacific. Metia, or Aurora Island, is one of the western Paumotus. It is a small island about four miles by two and a half in width, and two hundred and fifty feet in height; and it consists throughout of coral limestone. As we approached it from the northeast, its high vertical cliffs were supposed to be basaltic, and had much resemblance to the Palisades of the Hudson.† This appearance of a vertical structure was afterwards traced to vertical furrowings by the waters dripping down its front, and the consequent formation of stalagmitic incrustations. Deep caverns were also seen.

The cliff, though vertical in some parts, is roughly sloping in others, and on the west side, the surface of the island gradually declines to the sea.

The rock was found to be a white and solid limestone, seldom presenting any traces of its coral origin. In some few layers there were disseminated corals, looking like imbedded fossils, along with beautiful casts of shells; but for the most part it was as compact as any secondary marble, and as uniform in texture. Occasionally there were disseminated spots of crystallized calcspar.

The caverns presented us with coarse stalactites, some of which were six feet in diameter; and interesting specimens were obtained containing recent land shells, which had been enclosed while hibernating.‡

---

channels are narrow, or few in number, although the lagoon be of great size and depth, (as in Suadiva,) there are no ring-formed reefs; where the channels are somewhat broader, the marginal portions of reef, and especially those close to the larger channels are ring-formed, but the central ones are not so: where they are broadest, almost every reef throughout the atoll is more or less perfectly ring-formed. Although their presence is thus contingent on the openness of the marginal channels, the theory of their formation, as we shall hereafter see, is included in that of the parent atolls, of which they form the separate portions."

* Darwin, op. cit., p. 39.

† For a sketch of this island, see Narrative Exp. Exp., vol. i, p. 338.

‡ It is probable that more extensive caverns would have been found, had there been more than a few hours for the examination of the island. The Rev. Mr. Williams, in his work on Missionary Enterprises in the Pacific, gives very interesting

The surface of the island is singularly rough, owing to erosion by rains. The paths that cross it wind through narrow passages among ragged needles and ridges of rock as high as the head, the peaks and narrow defiles forming a miniature model of the grandest Alpine scenery. There is but little soil, yet the island is covered with trees and shrubbery.

The shores, at the first elevation of the island, must have been worn away to a large extent by the sea; and the cliff and some isolated pinnacles of coral rock still standing on the coast are evidence of the degradation. But at present there is a wide shore platform of coral reef, two hundred or two hundred and fifty feet wide, resembling that of the low coral islands, and having growing coral as usual about its margin and in the shallow depths beyond.

In the face of the cliff there are two horizontal lines, along which cavities or caverns are most frequent, which consequently give an appearance of stratification to the rock, dividing it into three nearly equal layers.

We might continue this account of coral reefs and islands, by particular descriptions of those visited by the Expedition. But the similarity among them is so great, and their peculiarities are already so fully detailed, that this would amount only to a succession of repetitions. And moreover the facts will be found in the geographical report by Captain Wilkes, and are to a great extent well exhibited on the map of the Paumotus and on the other valuable charts of the Expedition. The characters of a few briefly stated will suffice in this place. We commence with the smallest.

Jarvis's Island.—(Fig. 4, page 23.) Lat. 0° 22′ S. Long. 159° 31′ W. Length 1¾ miles trending east and west. No lagoon. Shape triangular. A low sandy flat, eighteen or twenty feet high, without trees, and partly covered with small shrubs. A high sloping beach continuous around. Trends east and west. We did not land on this island.

Birnie's.—Lat. 3° 35′ S. Long. 171° 39′ W. Four-fifths of a mile by one-third, trending northwest. No lagoon. A sandy flat about ten feet high, except near the north-northeast extremity,

descriptions of caverns in the *elevated* coral rock of Atiu, one of the Hervey Group.* In one, he wandered two hours without finding a termination to its windings, passing through chambers with "fretwork ceilings of stalagmite and stalactite columns, which, 'mid the darkness, sparkled brilliantly with the reflected torch-light." This author remarks, "that while the madrepores, the brain, and every other species of coral are full of little cells, these islands, (including those resembling Atiu,) appear to be *solid masses of compact limestone, in which nothing like a cell can be detected.*"

Beechey, in his description of Henderson Island, another of this character, speaks of the rock as *compact, and having the fracture of a secondary limestone.*

* Wateoo of Cook.

where it is about twelve feet. To the south-southwest the submerged reef extends out nearly a mile, over which the sea breaks. Distinguished no vegetation except the low purslane and some trailing plants. Did not land.

Swain's.—(Fig. 3, page 23.) Lat. 11° 10′ S. Long. 170° 52′ W. 1¼ miles by ⅝; shape nearly rectangular; trends east and west. No lagoon, but the centre a little lower than the sides. Surface covered with shrubbery and large trees, among the latter many cocoanuts; the centre more sparsely wooded. Height fifteen to eighteen feet, excepting on the middle of western side, where the surface is covered with loose fragments of coral of small size; there appears to have been a former entrance to the lagoon at this place. Shore reef or platform, one hundred yards in average width, and one hundred and fifty yards at the place where we landed. Beach high, ten to twelve feet. At lower part of beach for a height of two to three feet, the coral reef rock was exposed, indicating an elevation of the island. For three or four feet above this, layers of the beach sandrock were often in view, consisting of coral pebbles firmly cemented, and having the usual dip of seven or eight degrees seaward; in many places it was concealed by the beach sands and pebbles. There was no growing coral on the platform excepting Nullipores. The outer margin of this platform was very uneven, and much intersected by channels, though less so than at Enderby's Island.* Great numbers of Birgi, (large Crustacea,) were burrowing over the island, some of which were six inches in breadth.

Otuhu, Paumotu Archipelago.—14° 5′ S. 141° 30′ W. 1½ miles by ⅝, trending north and south. No lagoon. Wooded.

Margaret, Paumotu Archipelago.—20° 42′ S. 143° 4′ W. Diameter one mile, nearly circular. A small shallow lagoon with no entrance. Northeast side alone wooded, and in two patches.

Teku or *Four Crowns*, Paumotu Archipelago.—20° 28′ S. 143° 18′ W. Diameter 1½ miles, nearly circular. A small lagoon with no entrance. Southwestern reef bare; five patches of forest on the other part.

---

* The sea was quite heavy when we attempted to land at low tide upon the edge of the shore platform. As we pulled towards the reef, an anchor was dropped, as usual, some distance out, to hold on and save the boat, from being carried by the surges against the rocks. After some heavy seas had passed, a partial lull seemed to favor, and the boat was pulled in. Taking advantage of the favorable moment, I jumped out, and made rapid speed over the reef to escape the breakers which followed. Soon turning about, I was surprised to find the boat just behind me, and the crew in the water alongside trying to steady her and save her from destruction. The man who held to the anchor behind had let go his hold, and the next sea, as it came careering on, had borne the boat over the edge of the reef, and far on its surface. With even greater risk, after our ramble was completed, we succeeded in launching again and reached the open sea. This was one of many similar dangers experienced in these seas.

Washington Island.—Lat. 4° 41′ N. Long. 160° 15′ W. 3 miles by 1¼, trending east and west. It is a dense cocoanut grove with luxuriant shrubbery. No lagoon. The shore platform is rather narrow. A point of submerged reef one and a half miles long stretches out from southwest end. Could not land on account of bad weather.

Enderby's.—3° 8′ S. 171° 16′ W. 2¾ miles by 1 mile nearly, trending N. N. W. and S. S. E.; form trapezoidal or nearly rectangular. Little vegetation on any part, and but few trees. The lagoon very shallow and containing no growing coral; its shores a coral mud, allowing the foot to sink in eight or ten inches, and covered in places with saline incrustations. Shore platform one hundred feet or less in width, and surface inclined outward at a very small angle; covered with three or four feet of water at high tide, and with few corals or shells; beyond this, falls off four to six feet, and then the bottom gradually inclines for one hundred yards or more. The beach very high and regular; rises eight feet, at an inclination of thirty to thirty-five degrees; then horizontal for eighty to two hundred, after which another rise of three or four feet. It consists below of pebbles and fine sand, but above of slabs and blocks of coral rock and the beach sand-rock, those of the latter nearly rectangular and flat. This beach sandrock occurs in layers from ten to twenty inches thick along the shore, and is inclined from five to seven degrees seaward. Some portions are very compact, and ring under the hammer, while others enclose fragments of different sizes to a foot or more in diameter. The most common coral of the beach was an Astræa with small cells, (near A. cerium, D.—the specimens were afterwards lost.) There were also other Astræas, a large lamellar Madrepore, (M. cyclopea,) some fragments of which were six feet square and three inches thick; also Meandrinæ, Porites, &c. Large trunks of transported trees lay upon the island, one of which was forty feet long and four in diameter. The shore platform was much intersected by channels.

Captain Hudson obtained soundings half a mile off in two hundred fathoms; the lead struck upon a sandy bottom but was indented by coral.

Honden, or *Henuake,* Paumotu Archipelago.—Size 3½ miles by 2 miles. Oblong, five-sided; trending west-northwest. A small shallow lagoon, communicating with the sea only at high tide, on the west side. There are two other entrances, which are seldom if ever covered with water, and appeared merely as dry beds of coral rock. Height of the island, twelve feet: lowest on the south side. Belt of verdure complete, and consisting of large forest trees, with the Pandanus and other species, but no cocoanuts; its breadth ½ mile, and in some parts ¾. Among the trees, large masses of coral rock often exposed to view, and the surface in many parts very rough. It seemed surprising at all these islands to find so luxuriant a growth of trees and shrubbery over so rocky a surface. Shores of the lagoon nearly flat. On one side there was a large area of extremely fine coral sand and mud, which extended a long distance into the lagoon. Elsewhere about the centre of the island, the reef-rock was bare, and contained numerous shells of Tridacnæ. A few small Madrepores still growing in the lagoon. Beach on the sea-shore side eight feet high. In lower part of beach, several layers of white limestone, (the beach sandrock,) formed of coral fragments or sand, shells, &c., much of which was very compact. The layers inclined towards the sea at an angle of about five degrees. Shore platform as elsewhere in this archipelago.

The facts above stated are evidence of a slight elevation, not exceeding two or three feet.

Taiara, or *King's*, Paumotu Archipelago.—15° 42′ S.; 144° 46′ W. 2⅝ miles by 1¾, trending northwest. A small lagoon with no entrance. Reef almost continuously wooded around, somewhat broken into patches.

Maraki, Tarawan or Kingsmills Group.—5 miles by 2, and having a lagoon. Trending north. Shape oblong triangular. Belt of forest complete. Appearance of a former entrance to the lagoon on the east side.

Whytuhu, one of the two Disappointment Islands, Paumotu Archipelago.—14° 10′ S., 141° 24′ W. 5½ by 2 miles, trending northwest. The reef fronting northeast almost continuously wooded. On the opposite side, three islets, one of rather large size. Lagoon with no entrance.

Sydney Island.—Lat 4° 20′ S. Long. 171° 15′ W. Trends northeast and southwest. Well wooded nearly all round; but on leeward side the forest in patches, with breaks of bare coral. Lagoon narrow, without entrance. Width of island from sea to lagoon, one hundred to four hundred yards: width greatest at south end. Beach ten feet high. The soil of the island consisted of coral fragments and sand. Shore platform fifty to eighty feet wide; five or six feet water over it at high tide. Cut up very irregularly by channels three to eight or ten feet wide. Observed small corals growing on the bottom outside of the platform. Shores of lagoon shallow for fifty yards, and consisting of coral sand. Beyond this a slope covered with growing corals. The corals rather tender species of Madrepores. In the interior of the lagoon many knolls and large patches of coral.

Duke of York's.—8° 38′ S., 172° 27′ W. Form irregularly oblong, trending northwest. Length 3¾ miles; breadth 2 miles. Circuit 9½ miles, and about one half wooded in patches. Southwest reef mostly bare. A lagoon, but without entrance except for canoes at high tide, on leeward side. Island ten feet high.

Shore platform narrow, and intersected by channels. Shores lined by reef-rock, two or three feet out of water, indicating an elevation of the island. This reef-rock consists of various corals firmly cemented. Within the lagoon, knolls of coral, but none near the shore on the leeward side.

Fakaafo or *Bowditch's.*—9° 20′ S., 171° 5′ W. 6¾ miles by 4. Shape nearly triangular. Circuit seventeen miles, about six of which are wooded in several patches, separated by long bare intervals. A large lagoon, but no ship entrance. Height of island, fifteen feet. Width to the lagoon, one hundred to two hundred yards. Soil of the island coral sand, speckled black with results of vegetable decomposition. Shore platform narrow. At outer edge a depth of three fathoms, and from thence gradually deepens, and abounds in fine corals for fifty yards, when it deepens abruptly. Coral reef-rock elevated three or four feet, indicating an elevation of the island. Lagoon shallow, with some growing coral, but none near the shore. Some corals growing on the platform, near its margin, mostly small Madrepores, Astræas, Nullipores. Fragments of pumice were found among the natives, which had floated to the island.

Ahii, or *Peacock's Island*, Paumotu Archipelago.—14° 30′ S., 146° 20′ W. 13 miles by 6, trending N. E. by E. Shape irregularly oblong. A large lagoon, having an entrance for small vessels on the west. Reef wooded throughout nearly its whole circuit. Lagoon shallow, and much obstructed by growing coral, the latter giving the water over it a clear light green color. Platform, or outer coral shelf of the island, about two hundred and fifty feet wide; under water except at the lowest tides. Margin highest, and covered with Nullipore incrustations, which give it a variety of delicate shades of color, mostly reddish, or peach-blossom red, rose, scarlet. For thirty to fifty feet from the margin, very cavernous, and containing many Tridacnæ, lying half imbedded, with the variously tinted mantle expanded when the surface is covered with water. Rock of the platform either a compact white limestone or a solid conglomerate; dead over its surface, excepting a few Madrepore tufts or Astræas near the margin in pools. In this shelf there were long fissures, extending nearly parallel with the shore, a quarter to half an inch wide at top, and continuing sometimes a fourth of a mile or more. These fissures were commonly filled with coral sand. The higher parts of the island either consisting of loose blocks of coral or covered with some soil; the soil mostly of comminuted coral and shells, with dark particles from vegetable decomposition intermingled. On the bottom exterior to the shore platform, observed the same corals growing as occurred in fragments upon the island; but the larger part of the bottom was without coral, or consisted only of sand.

Raraka, Paumotu Archipelago.—16° 10′ S., 145° W. 14 miles by 8, trending east and west. Shape somewhat triangular. North side nearly continuously wooded: south angle and southwest reef bare. A large lagoon with an entrance for small vessels on the north side. A rapid current flows from the entrance, which it was difficult for a boat to pull against. Shore platform, as usual, about a hundred yards wide, with the edge rather higher than the surface back; the platform mostly bare of water at low tide. Several large masses of coral and coral rock, one to four hundred cubic feet, on the platform and upon the higher parts of the island, some of which stood five and six feet above high-water mark; they were cemented to the reef-rock below, and appeared like projecting parts of the reef. Layers of beach sandrock on the lagoon shores, as well as on the seaward side, inclined at an angle of six or seven degrees: characters as already described. Growing coral in the entrance to the lagoon, within two feet of the surface, mostly a species of Millepora, (M. squarrosa.) Interior of the lagoon not examined for want of time. The water looked as blue as the ocean, and was much roughened by the winds.

Kawehe, or *Vincennes Island*, Paumotu Archipelago, 15° 30′ S., 145° 10′ W. 13 miles by 9, trending north-northwest. Shape irregularly oval. Having a large lagoon, and mostly wooded around, least so to leeward. Between the wooded islets, (as on Raraka and elsewhere,) surface consisted of angular masses of coral rock, (among which the Porites prevail,) strewed in great numbers together; and in some parts bearing a few vines and purslane among the blocks, though scarcely any appearance of soil, or even of coral sand. In other parts, not as high, no vegetation, and surface still wet by high tide. A few large masses of coral on the shore platform, either lying loose, or firmly attached below; some of them were six feet cube, and one was raised seven feet above high-water mark. Those that were attached were so firmly cemented to the reef-rock as to seem to be a part of it, and they were partly worn off below by the wash of the sea; the surface was extremely rough, owing to wear by rains. These masses were sometimes single individual corals, and others were conglomerate in character. Shore platform about a hundred yards wide, rather highest at the edge, and much of its surface two to four feet under water at low tide. As elsewhere, this platform is nothing but a compact coral conglomerate or limestone, having no growing coral over it, except in some shallow pools near its outer margin, where also there are numerous holes in which crabs are concealed, with small fish and other animals of the shores. On the lagoon shore, layers of beach sandrock, six or seven in number, dipping at an angle of seven degrees towards the lagoon, and outcropping one from beneath the other. Similar layers on the sea-shore side.

Manhii, Wilson's or *Waterlandt*, Paumotu Archipelago, 14° 25′ S., 146° W. 15 miles by 6, trending E.N.E. A large lagoon with a deep entrance on the west side. Shape oblong triangular.

Shore platform as usual; mostly under water at low tide. Large masses of coral here and there, standing on this reef, either cemented to it or loose. One top-shaped mass is figured on p. 29. High water did not reach the part of it which was most worn; and this was evidently owing to the fact that the action of the swell, or waves, is greatest above the actual level of the tide at the time. This mass was not of fragmentary composition; it was apparently the remains of a single individual Porites. Another loose mass was five and a half feet high, and averaged ten feet across, (fig. 3, p. 30.) It consisted of large masses of Astræas, Madrepores, and Porites cemented together, and contained imbedded shells, an Astræa, Cypræa, &c. The reef-rock is either a compact limestone showing no traces of its composite origin, or a conglomerate. Beach, regular as usual, 6 to 10 feet high, consisting of coral sand, and fragments of worn shells, with occasional exuviæ of crabs, remains of Echini, fish, &c. The entrance to the lagoon is deep and narrow, with vertical sides.

Aratica or *Carlshoff*, Paumotu Archipelago, 15° 30′ S., 145° 30′ W. 17 miles by 10, trending N. E. Large lagoon, with a good entrance for vessels. The reef fronting south, bare for nine miles: on northwest side, mostly very low, with only here and there a clump of trees; occasionally a line of wooded land for a quarter of a mile on the east side; more continuously wooded on the north. The bare parts, mostly covered with blocks of coral, 1 to 30 cubic feet, and larger, tumbled together, as on the preceding. Some blocks of coral on the shore platform very large; one 8 feet high and 15 in diameter, containing at least 1000 cubic feet; it lay on the reef and was not connected with it; below it, the platform was 6 inches higher than the surface either side, owing to the action of the sea. These blocks are in all instances rough angular, and appear as if they had been thrown up by the sea, and left exposed to wear from the rains and spray.

Nairsa or *Dean's*, Paumotu Archipelago, 15° S., 148° W. 44 miles by 17, trending W. N. W. Northern shore mostly wooded; southern with only an occasional islet, connected by long lines of bare reef. In these intervals, the reef stood eight feet or so out of water, and was worn into a range of columns, or excavated with caverns, so as to look very much broken, though quite regularly even in the level of the top line.

We might continue these descriptions; but the above, with the details before given, will convey a general idea of the whole.

C. The Completed Coral Island.

The coral island in its best condition is but a miserable residence for man. There is poetry in every feature: but the natives find this a poor substitute for the breadfruit and yams of more favored lands. The cocoanut and Pandanus are, in general, the only products of the vegetable kingdom afforded for their sustenance, and fish and crabs from the reefs their only animal food. Scanty too is the supply; and infanticide is resorted to in self-defence, where but a few years would otherwise overstock the half-a-dozen square miles of which their little world consists.

Yet there are more comforts than might be expected on a land of so limited extent,—without rivers, without hills, in the midst of salt water, with the most elevated point but ten feet above high tide, and no part more than 300 yards from the ocean. Though the soil is light and the surface often strewed with blocks of coral, there is a dense covering of vegetation to shade the native villages from a tropical sun. The cocoanut, the tree of a thousand uses, grows luxuriantly on the coral-made land, after it has emerged from the ocean; and the scanty dresses of the natives, their drinking vessels and other utensils, mats, cordage, fishing-lines, and oil, besides food, drink, and building material, are all supplied from it. The Pandanus or screw-pine flourishes well, and is exactly fitted for such regions: as it enlarges and spreads its branches, one prop after another grows out from the trunk and plants itself in the ground; and by this means its base is widened and the growing tree supported. The fruit, a large ovoidal mass made up of oblong dry seed, diverging from a centre, each near two cubic inches in size, affords a sweetish husky article of food, which, though little better than prepared corn stalks, admits of being stored away for use when other things fail. The extensive reefs, abound in fish which are easily captured, and the natives, with wooden hooks, often bring in larger kinds from the deep waters. From such resources a population of 10,000 persons is supported on the single island of Taputeouea, whose whole habitable area does not exceed six square miles.*

Water is to be found commonly in sufficient quantities for the use of the natives, although the land is so low and flat. They dig wells five to ten feet deep in any part of the dry islets, and generally obtain a constant supply. These wells are sometimes fenced around with special care; and the houses of the villagers, as at Fakaafo, are often clustered about them. On Aratica (Carls-

---

* There are a few islands better supplied with vegetable food, though the above statements are literally true of a large majority.

hoff) there is a watering place 50 feet in diameter, from which our vessels in a few hours obtained 390 gallons. The Tarawan Islands are generally provided with a supply sufficient for bathing, and each native takes his morning bath in fresh water, which is esteemed by them a great luxury. On Taritari, as Mr. Hale was informed by a Scotch sailor taken from the island, by the name of Gray, there is a long trench or canal, described by him as several miles long, and two feet deep. They have *taro* plantations, which require a large supply of water, besides some bread-fruit. These islands have been elevated a little, but are not over fifteen feet above the sea.*

The only source of this water, is the rains, which, percolating through the loose surface, settle upon the hardened coral rock that forms the basis of the island. As the soil is white or nearly so, it receives heat but slowly, and there is consequently but little evaporation of the water that is once absorbed.

These islands moreover enclose ports of great extent, many admitting even the largest class of vessels: and the same lagoons are the pearl fisheries of the Pacific.

An occasional log drifts to their shores, and at some of the more isolated atolls, where the natives are ignorant of any land but the spot they inhabit, they are deemed direct gifts from a propitiated deity. These drift-logs were noticed by Kotzebue, at the Marshall Islands, and he remarked also that they often brought stones in their roots. Similar facts were observed by us at the Tarawan Group, and also at Enderby's Island and elsewhere.

The stones at the Tarawan Islands, as far as we could learn, are generally basaltic, and they are highly valued for whetstones, pestles, and hatchets. The logs are claimed by the chiefs for canoes. Some of the logs, like those at Enderby's Island, were forty feet or more long.

Fragments of pumice and resin are transported by the waves to the Tarawan Islands. We were informed that the pumice was gathered from the shores by the women, and pounded up to fertilize the soil of their taro patches; and it is so common that one woman will pick up a peck in a day. Pumice was also met

---

* The Scotchman (Gray) from whom this information was obtained, added that ten ships of the line might water there, though the place was not reached without some difficulty. There were fish in the pond which had been put in while young. The bottom was adhesive like clay. He spoke of the taro as growing to a very large size, and as being in great abundance; it was planted along each side of the pond.

Kotzebue observes, that "in the inner part of Otdia [one of the Marshall Islands] there is a lake of sweet water; and in Tabual, of the group Aur, a marshy ground exists. There is no want of fresh water in the larger islands; it rises in abundance in the pits dug for the purpose." *Voyage*, London, 1821, iii, 145.

with at Fakaafo. Volcanic ashes are sometimes distributed over these islands, through the atmosphere; and in this manner the soil of the Tonga Islands is improved, and in some places it has received a reddish color.

The officers of the Vincennes observed several large masses of compact and cellular basalt on Rose Island, a few degrees east of Samoa: they were lying two hundred yards inside of the line of breakers. The island is uninhabited, and the origin of the stones is doubtful; they may have been brought there by roots of trees, or perhaps by some canoe.

Notwithstanding the great number of coral islands in the Paumotu Archipelago, the botanist finds there, as Dr. Pickering informs me, only twenty-eight or twenty-nine native species of plants. The following are the most common of them:—

Portulacca, two species.
Scævola Konigii.
Pisonia? one species.
Tournefortia sericea.
Pandanus odoratissimus.
Lepidium, one species.
Euphorbia, one species.
Morinda citrifolia.
Boerhavia, two species.
Cassytha, one species.
Heliotropium prostratum.
Pemphis acidula.
Guettarda speciosa.
Triumphetta procumbens.
Suriana maritima?
Convolvulus, one species.
Urtica, one or two species.
Asplenium nidus.
Achyranthus, one species.
A species of grass.
One or two rubiaceous shrubs.
Polypodium.

On Rose Island Dr. Pickering found only the *Pisonia* and a *Portulacca*. The *Triumphetta procumbens*, a creeping plant, takes root like the Portulacca, in the most barren sands, and is very common. The *Tournefortia* and *Scævola* are also among the earliest species. The *Pisonia*, a tree of handsome foliage, the *Pandanus* or Screw-pine, and the *Cocoanut*, (always an introduced species,) constitute the larger part of the forests. In the Marshall Group, where the vegetation is more varied, Chamisso observed fifty-two native plants, and in a few instances the Banana, Taro, and Breadfruit.

The language of the natives indicates their poverty, as well as the limited productions and unvarying features of the land. All words like those for mountain, hill, river, and many of the implements of their ancestors, as well as the trees and other vegetation of the land from which they are derived, are lost to them; and as words are but signs for ideas, they have fallen off in general intelligence. It would be an interesting inquiry for the philosopher, to what extent a race of men placed in such circumstances are capable of mental improvement. Perhaps the query might be best answered by another, How many of the various arts of civilized life could exist in a land, where shells are the only cutting instruments,—the plants in all but twenty-nine in number,—but a single mineral,—quadrupeds none, with the exception of foreign mice,—fresh water barely enough for household purposes,—no streams, nor mountains, nor hills? How much of the poetry or literature of Europe would be intelligible to persons whose ideas had expanded only to the limits of a coral island;—who had never conceived of a surface of land above half a mile in breadth,—of a slope higher than a beach,—of a change of seasons beyond a variation in the prevalence of rains? What elevation in morals should be expected upon a contracted islet, so readily over-peopled that threatened starvation drives to infanticide, and tends to cultivate the extremest selfishness? Assuredly there is not a more unfavorable spot for moral or intellectual development in the wide world than the coral island, with all its beauty of grove and lake.

These islands are exposed to earthquakes and storms like the continents, and occasionally a devastating wave sweeps across the land. During the heavier gales, the natives sometimes secure their houses by tying them to the cocoanut trees, or to a stake planted for the purpose. A height of ten or twelve feet, the elevation of their land, is easily overtopped by the more violent seas; and great damage is sometimes experienced. The still more extensive earthquake-waves, such as those which have swept up the coast of Spain, Peru, and the Sandwich Islands, would produce a complete deluge over these islands. We were informed by both Gray and Kirby, that effects of this kind had been experienced at the Tarawan Islands; but the statements were too indefinite to determine whether the results should be attributed to storms or to this more violent cause.

The preceding pages have been occupied with a simple description of the actual condition, structure, and appearances of reefs and reef islands. From this review of their existing features, we may pass on to the consideration of those agencies by which these features were produced, tracing out the steps in the progress of such formations, and the influence of various causes on their forms and distribution. We may commence with a brief account of the living zoophyte, its habits and its mode of growth,—as some knowledge on these points is essential to the correct appreciation of the discussion before us. This branch of the subject has been treated of at length in another volume, to which reference may be made for fuller details.*

* Report on Zoophytes, by the author.

CHAPTER II.

STRUCTURE, GROWTH, AND HABITS OF CORAL ZOOPHYTES.

1. *Structure and Growth of Zoophytes.*

A SINGULAR degree of obscurity has been thrown around the growth of coral zoophytes and coral formations, through the various speculations which have been offered in place of facts; and to the present day, the subject is seldom mentioned without the qualifying adjective *mysterious* expressed or understood. Some writers, scouting the idea that reefs of rocks can be due in any way to "animalcules," talk of electrical forces, the first and last appeal of ignorance. Others call in the fishes of the seas, suggesting that they are the masons, and work with their teeth in the accumulation of the calcareous material. Very many of those who discourse quite learnedly on zoophytes and reefs, imagine that the polyps are mechanical workers, heaping up these piles of rock by their united labors; and science still retains such terms as polypary, polypidom, as if each coral were the constructed hive or house of a swarm of polyps, like the honeycomb of the bee, or the hillock of a colony of ants.

It is vain to hope to understand fully the works of Him who is himself infinite and incomprehensible. The scrutinizing eye of science penetrates with far-reaching sight the system of things about us, and in the dim limits of vision reads everywhere the word mystery. All life, animal and vegetable, and all that is inanimate, declare it; surely there is no special reason, except such as may arise from want of study and consideration, for attributing it pre-eminently to the humblest grades of existence.

It is not more surprising nor a matter of more difficult comprehension that the polyp should form coral, than that the quadruped should form its bones, or the mollusc its shell. The processes are similar, and so the result: in each case it is a simple animal secretion, a formation of stony matter from the aliment which the animal receives, produced by certain parts of the animal fitted for this secreting process. This power of secretion is the first and most common of those that belong to living tissues; and though differing in different organs according to their end or function, it is all one process, both in nature or cause, whether in the animalcule or in man. Coral is never, therefore, an agglutination of grains made by the handywork of the many-armed polyps: for it is no more an act of labor than bone-making in ourselves. And again, it is not a collection of cells into which the coral animals may withdraw for concealment, any more than the skeleton of a dog is its house or cell: for every part of the coral of a polyp in most reef-making species is enclosed *within* the polyp, where it was formed by the secreting process.*

It is important that this point should be thoroughly understood, and fully appreciated. That error may no longer be perpetuated, the words polypary and the like, have been rejected by the author in his volume on Zoophytes, and the more familiar term *corallum* has been used instead.† With this introductory explanation, we proceed.

a. Structure of Coral Animals or Polyps.—A good idea of a coral polyp may be had from comparison with the garden aster: for the likeness in external form and delicacy of coloring is singularly close. The aster consists of a tinted disk bordered with one or more series of petals; and in exact analogy, the polyp-flower, in its most common form, has a disk often richly colored, fringed around with petal-like organs called tentacles. Below the disk, in contrast with the slender pedicel of the plant, there is a stout cylindrical pedicel or body, often as broad as the disk itself, and usually not much longer, which contains the *stomach* and internal cavity of the polyp: and the *mouth*, which opens into the stomach, is placed at the centre of the disk. Here, then, the flower-animal and the garden-flower diverge in character, the difference being required by the different modes of nutrition in the two kingdoms of nature.

There are many species of polyps, which have all the external and internal characters of coral polyps, yet secrete no lime or coral. Our descriptions of structure may be best drawn from them, and afterwards the single peculiarity of the coral-making polyp—its secretion of coral—will come under consideration. The species here referred to are called *Actiniæ* in science, in allusion to the radiated or aster-like flower which forms the summit of the animal.‡ There is the same allusion in the common appellation *Sea-anemone.* The richest anemones, daisies and tulips of our gardens would not rival them in beauty, neither will

---

* It is not, perhaps, within the range of science to criticise the poet; yet we may say in this place, in view of the frequent use of the lines even by scientific men, that more error in the same compass could scarcely be found than in the part of Montgomery's Pelican Island, relating to coral formations. The poetry is beautiful, the facts nearly all errors—if literature allows of such an incongruity. For ourselves, we think the poet transcends his appropriate limits when false to nature.

† See page 15, of the Report on Zoophytes. The term Corallium has been set aside by authors because of its being used for a genus of corals. *Corallum* is an old form of the same word, as particularly explained on the page just referred to, and is not liable to this objection. The true nature of calcareous corals was first pointed out by Milne Edwards and Ehrenberg.

‡ From ακτιν, *a ray of the sun.*

they exceed them in the size of their flowers; for a breadth of two and three inches is common. The polyps here alluded to, along with the coral polyps allied, constitute the order or division of zoophytes called ACTINOIDEA.*

The Actiniæ are entirely fleshy, and usually live attached by their lower extremity to the submerged rocks of the shores. The mouth, at the centre of the flower-like disk forming the summit of the animal, is a simple opening without teeth or appendages of any kind. The tentacles—the petals of the flower—are tubular organs, and communicate internally with the interior cavity of the animal. The animal contracts, when disturbed, and conceals the flower by rolling inward over it the margin bearing the tentacles; and in this state it seems like a lifeless lump of animal matter. Left quiet for a while, it again expands and appears as before. This expansion is produced by receiving water into the interior from without, mostly through the mouth, and thus filling the tentacles and swelling out its fleshy body. They are generally found expanded with the mouth wide open to receive their prey. As they are fixed to the rocks, they must wait for their food to come to them. When a crab, shell-fish, or anything alive, within the capabilities of their bodies, comes within reach, they usually secure it by closing upon the victim the tentacles, (which commonly have a stinging power,) and pushing it into the mouth. In many species the tentacles are too short to aid in capturing food except it be by stinging. These organs subserve also the purpose of aerating the blood, a function in which all parts of the body are more or less concerned.

The interior of the actinia contains a cylindrical stomach suspended from the disk, which opens at bottom into the general cavity of the body. This general cavity, below the stomach and around it, is divided into compartments by radiating fleshy lamellæ, the larger of which in their upper part connect the stomach with the sides of the animal. The most important function of these lamellæ is that of reproduction, some being spermatic, and the others bearing clusters of ova. These ova leave the body by passing out through the stomach and mouth; but in many instances this does not take place till the young animal has proceeded from them. The refuse from the food after digestion in the stomach is also ejected by the mouth, as this is the only opening to the alimentary cavity. Other excrementitious matters, separated on the final elaboration of the chyle and its assimilation, may escape through the sides of the animal, the openings at the extremities of the tentacles, or in general by whatever pores or passages water may be ejected in the contraction of the animal.

* This term alludes to their general resemblance to Actiniæ.

One of the most singular peculiarities of polyps is their ready restoration of a lost part. Even a fragment will go on to complete the entire animal again: as with the fabled hydra of old, the knife is used but to multiply, for every section becomes a new animal.

In all the points mentioned in the description here given, the polyp of ordinary coral and the actinia are identical.

b. Process of Budding.—There is one mode of reproduction which, although having no necessary connection with coral secretions, belongs almost exclusively to coral polyps. This is *reproduction by buds;* and the process is so similar to the production of buds in vegetation, that a remembrance of the latter will aid much in conceiving of it. The bud generally commences as a slight prominence on the side of the parent: the prominence enlarges, and soon a circle of tentacles grows out, with a mouth at the centre; enlargement goes on till the young finally equals the parent in size. Thus by budding, a compound group is commenced; and it is evident that if the parent and the new polyp go on budding again, and so on, the compound group may continue to enlarge. This is the fact in nature. The polyps, one and all, continue propagating by buds, until in some instances thousands, or hundreds of thousands, have proceeded from a single one, and the colony has spread to a large size. Such is the Madrepora and Astræa. There are modifications of this process, analogous to those in vegetation, but we need not dwell upon them in this place.

It is obvious that the connection of the polyps in such a compound group must be of the most intimate kind. The several polyps have separate mouths and tentacles, and separate stomachs; but beyond this there is no individual property. They coalesce, or are one, by intervening tissues, and there is a free circulation of fluids through the many pores or lacunes. The zoophyte is like a living sheet of animal matter, fed and nourished by numerous mouths and as many stomachs. In some species the coalescence is confined to the lower half of the polyps, or to a still less part; and in this case the animals project above the general living surface. Polyps thus clustered, spreading at summit a star of tentacles, constitute the flowering zoophytes of coral reefs.

Those coral animals which do not bud are to all external appearance true actiniæ. The existence of coral in the living coral zoophyte is nowhere apparent, and would not be suspected if not previously known; for, as before stated, it is wholly internal, and the visible exterior is the fleshy skin of the polyp.

c. Secretion of Coral.—We have already remarked on the general nature of coral secretions. These secretions, it should be farther observed, increase within simultaneously with growth, and every new animal adds to those previously formed. They go on throughout the sides and base of each polyp, excepting generally the exterior skin, as above stated; and the whole forms a calcareous framework penetrated by the animal tissues, some of these tissues corresponding to and occupying the cellules of the corallum, and others penetrating the solid parts in minute ramifications. Coral is also secreted between the radiating fleshy lamellæ of the internal cavity of the polyp, producing the radiated calcareous lamellæ which constitute the star of a cell. In the corallum of a Madrepora or an Astræa each surface cell or star belonged to a separate polyp, and the star was formed as here explained.

It would lead to too long a digression from the main topic before us to explain the principles upon which the forms of zoophytes depend. They are dwelt upon at length in another volume. In this place we may briefly allude to the principal varieties of form proceeding from the budding process, and to a single point in their mode of growth, upon which much of their importance in reef-making depends.

d. Forms of Actinoid Zoophytes.—Zoophytes imitate nearly every variety of vegetation. Trees of coral are well known; and although not emulating in size the oaks of our forests,—for they do not exceed six or eight feet in height,—they are gracefully branched, and the whole surface blooms with coral polyps in place of leaves and flowers. Shrubbery, tufts of rushes, beds of pinks, and feathery mosses, are most exactly imitated. Many species spread out in broad leaves or folia, and resemble some large-leaved plant just unfolding: when alive, the surface of each leaf is covered with polyp flowers. The cactus, the lichen clinging to the rock, and the fungus in all its varieties, have their numerous representatives. Besides these forms imitating vegetation, there are gracefully modelled vases, some of which are three or four feet in diameter, made up of a network of branches and branchlets and sprigs of flowers. There are also solid coral hemispheres like domes among the vases and shrubbery, occasionally ten, or even twenty feet in diameter, whose symmetrical surface is gorgeously decked with polyp-stars of purple and emerald green.*

All the many shapes proceed in each instance from a single germ, which grows and buds under a few simple laws of development, and thus gives origin either to the branch, the broad leaf, the column, or the hemisphere.

e. Life and Death in Concurrent Progress.—But the more massy forms would not exist, and others would be of diminutive

* See Report on Zoophytes, pp. 29 and 59–61.

size, were it not for a peculiar mode of growth which characterizes most coral zoophytes.

Life and death are here in concurrent or parallel progress, a condition favored by the existence of coral secretions. In some instances, a simple polyp, while growing at top and constantly lengthening itself upward, is dying at its lower extremity, leaving the base of the coral bare, and destitute of any living tissues. The polyp thus continues rising in height, and death progresses below at the same rate, till at last the live polyp may be at the extremity of a coral stem many times its own length. This process is illustrated by figures on pages 62 and 78 of the Report on Zoophytes.

In species which bud and form large groups, the same operation takes place. In some instances the summit polyp or polyps bud and grow, while at a certain distance below the summit, the work of death is going on and polyps are gradually disappearing. There is thus a certain interval of life, the length of which interval is different for different species. There are zoophytes which grow to a height of several feet, and still only the upper one or two inches are living. The recent polyps at the top of the column are active with life and vigorous in reproduction, while the more aged below, having reached the fixed limits of their existence, are disappearing. The enduring coral remains, and constitutes the basement or stage of action for future generations of polyps.

But this death is not in progress alone at the base of the column or branch. Generally the *whole interior* of a corallum is dead, a result of the same process with that just explained. Thus, a Madrepora, although the branch may be an inch in diameter, is alive only to a depth of a line or two, the growing polyps of the surface having progressively died at their lower or inner extremity as they increased outward.

The large domes of Astræas, which have been stated to attain sometimes a diameter of ten or twenty feet, and are alive over the whole surface, owing to a symmetrical and unlimited mode of budding, are nothing but lifeless coral throughout the interior. Could the living portion be separated, it would form a hemispherical shell of polyps, in most species about half an inch thick. In some Porites of the same size, the whole mass is lifeless, excepting the exterior for a sixth of an inch in depth.

With such a mode of increase, there is no necessary limit to the growth of zoophytes. The rising column may grow upward, until it nears the surface of the sea, when death ensues simply from exposure, and not from any failure in its powers of life. The huge domes may enlarge till the same exposure just mentioned causes the death of the summit, and leaves only the sides to grow, which may increase indefinitely. Moreover, it is evident that if the land supporting the growing coral were very gradually sinking, the upward increase of the coral might still be without limit.

There is hence sufficient means provided for the production of coral material for islands, however numerous. These humble ministers of creative power might, without other attributes than those they now possess, have laid the foundations of continents, and covered them with mountain ranges. This remark requires no limitation if we allow the requisite time, and connect with the power of growth such other agencies, soon to be explained, as have been at work in the Pacific since the reefs were there in progress.

The death of the polyps about the base of a coral tree would expose it seemingly to immediate wear from the waters around it, and especially as the texture is usually porous. But nature is not without an expedient to prevent a catastrophe that would be destructive to a large part of growing zoophytes, and would prevent the indefinite increase just explained. The dead surface becomes the resting-place of numberless small incrusting species of corals, besides Nullipores, Serpulas, and some molluscs. In many instances the lichen-like Nullipore grows at the same rate with the rate of death in the zoophyte, and keeps itself up to the very limit of the living part. The dead trunk of the forest becomes covered with lichens and fungi, or in tropical climes, with other foliage and various foreign flowers: so among the coral productions of the sea, there are forms of life which replace the dying polyp. The process of wear is thus entirely prevented.

The older polyps, before death, often increase their coral secretions within, filling the pores occupied by the tissues, and rendering the corallum more solid; and this is another means by which the trees of coral growth, though of slender form, are increased in strength and endurance.

The facility with which polyps repair a wound, aids in carrying forward the results above described. The breaking of a branch is no serious injury to a zoophyte. There is often some degree of sensibility apparent throughout a clump, even when of considerable size, and the shock, therefore, may occasion the polyps to close. But in an hour, or perhaps much less time, their tentacles will have again expanded; and such as were torn by the fracture will be in the process of complete restoration to their former size and powers. The fragment broken off, dropping in a favorable place, would become the germ of another coral plant, its base cementing by means of coral-secretions to the rock on which it might rest; or if still in contact with any part of the parent tree, it would be reunited and continue to grow as before. The coral zoophyte may be levelled by transported masses swept over by the waves; yet like the trodden sod, it sprouts again, and continues to grow and flourish as before. The sod, however, has roots which are still unhurt; while the zoophyte, which may be dead at base, has a root—a source or centre of life—in every polyp that blossoms over its surface. Each animal might live and grow if separated from the rest, and would ultimately produce a mature zoophyte.

We close this review of the characters of coral animals, which is a mere abstract of the fuller descriptions in the General Report on Zoophytes, by alluding briefly to a second division of Zoophytes, not yet touched upon, and also to the Hydroidea and Bryozoa, which are likewise coral-making animals.

THE ALCYONOIDEA.—The polyps of the Alcyonium* group of zoophytes differ from those which have been occupying us, in having but eight tentacles, and these are fringed with minute papillæ. The organ-pipe coral (Tubipora) is of this kind. When expanded in the sea, a clump resembles a bed of pinks, or looks like a lilac-cluster that had been dropped in the water; and this resemblance extends to the color and size of the flowers as well as their form.

Some of these zoophytes secrete lime and form a tube; and of this kind is the Tubipora. Others secrete only scattered granules of lime through the tissues: and still others are fleshy throughout. Many of them, besides forming granular calcareous secretions within the body of the polyp, give origin to a horny secretion at base, analogous to the epidermic secretions (hair, nails) of other animals; and this secretion receiving constant additions from the polyps as they are successively budded out, forms the axis of the growing branch. Of this character is the horny axis of the Gorgonia or sea-fan, which was long taken for a vegetable production. The crust which covers the axis consists of united polyps, which expand over its surface; and when expanded, each branch becomes a spike of flowers.

THE HYDROIDEA.—The Hydroidea include the groups Hydra, Sertularia, Tubularia and the allied. Some species form thready tufts and plumes of extreme delicacy and others (the Hydræ) are simple polyps. The fine branchlets of the feathery species consist when dead of one or two series of microscopic cells arranged like tiny cups, tubes or goblets along the stem; and when alive, each cell is the site of a minute flower-animal. A coronet of tentacles surrounds the mouth, as in the Actiniæ, though somewhat different in character. The internal cavity is a simple tube without radiating lamellæ or special organs of reproduction, and the gemmules grow out singly or in bunches from the sides of the

* This name is derived from Alcyone, the fabled daughter of Neptune, and although from a Greek word having the aspirate breathing to the first letter, it was usually written by the Latins as here, (and by Linnæus and others,) without the H.

animal. The Hydra, an animal a line or two in length, consists of a tubular body, with a mouth at one extremity surrounded by a circle of tentacles: and the structure of the animal is so simple that it may be turned inside out, and still live and eat; it may be cut into forty or more parts, and from the dissected body, will grow as many distinct Hydræ. The Hydroidea are all minute and act no important part in reef-making.

The Hydroidea were long considered mature animals. But recent investigations have shown that part at least develop Medusæ, which are properly the adult individuals since these alone produce true ova. This division has therefore been recently removed from the zoophytes and placed with the Acalephs or Jelly-fishes.

The Bryozoa.—The Bryozoa are other coral-making species; but they are related to certain molluscs called Ascidiæ rather than to zoophytes. In habit and size they much resemble the Hydroidea. From a minute cabin-like cell, they extend a circlet of slender arms or tentacles, and expand into a delicate goblet-shape flower, seldom over a line in diameter. These polyps differ both from the Actinoidea and Hydroidea, in having two extremities to the alimentary canal—an anus, as well as a mouth; the intestine curves around and terminates in the disk. They are widely removed from true zoophytes, both by this character, and also by having the tentacles furnished with vibratile cilia—that is, minute appendages resembling short hairs, which are kept in nearly constant vibration.

Some species of Bryozoa form thin crusts over rocks or seaweeds, consisting of united cells, scarcely distinguishable unless magnified. The coralla of other species are branching or thin foliaceous; and these also consist of series of minute cells.

2. *Texture and Composition of Corals.*

The *texture* of calcareous corals is in general quite porous or cellular. Small stars or rounded depressions are scattered over the surface, and sometimes these stars form the centres of small prominences, called calicles (little cups). Besides these polyp-cells, which mark the position each of a separate polyp, there are pores or cellules penetrating the texture of the coral mass; yet in some zoophytes, the coral secretions continue increasing in the animal till the pores are almost or quite obliterated, and the texture is nearly compact, the polyp cells alone remaining. In many species, wherever there are concavities of much depth in the surface of a zoophyte, the coral of these concavities is looser or more spongy than elsewhere, for the reason, apparently, that the polyps in such parts have a poorer chance for securing food and fresh portions of water.

In the Gorgoniæ, and other species forming a distinct axis to the branches, this axis is solid, without a trace of a cell, and usually with faint evidences of a concentric structure. It is thus that the red coral of commerce, used in jewelry, differs from the Madrepore or common white coral: it is the *axis* of a species of Corallium; and the polyps constituted a layer about it, in the same manner as the polyps of Gorgoniæ cover the horny axis of these species.

In *hardness*, the common calcareous corals are a little above ordinary limestone or marble, the degree being represented in the mineralogical scale of Mohs by 3·5 to 4, while, in limestone, it is about 3. The ringing sound given when coral is struck with a hammer, indicates this superior hardness. It is a common error of old date to suppose that coral when first removed from the water is soft, and afterwards hardens on exposure. But, in fact, there is scarcely an appreciable difference; the live coral has a slimy feel in the fingers; but if washed clear of the animal matter, it is found to be quite firm. The waters with which it is penetrated may contain a trace of lime in solution, which evaporates on drying, and adds slightly to the strength of the coral, but the change is hardly appreciable. A branched Madrepore rings on being struck when first collected; and a blow in any part puts in hazard every branch throughout it, on account of its elasticity and brittleness. Its *specific gravity* varies from 2·5 to 2·8: 2·523 was the average from fifteen specimens examined by Prof. B. Silliman, Jr.*

In *composition*, the common reef-corals, of which the branching Madrepora, and the massive Astræas are good examples, consist almost wholly of carbonate of lime, the same ingredient which constitutes ordinary limestone. In 100 parts, 90 to 96 parts are of this constituent; of the remainder, there are 3 to 8 parts of organic matter, with some earthy ingredients amounting in certain species to 2 parts, though often less than 1. These earthy ingredients are silica, magnesia, alumina, oxyd of iron, phosphate of magnesia, and fluorids of magnesium and calcium. The following is the result of one of Mr. Silliman's analyses from those made by him for the Report on Zoophytes.† The specimen was a Porites from the Sandwich Islands. It afforded—

Carbonate of lime, ...	95·84
Phosphates, fluorids, &c., . .	2·05
Organic matter, ...	2·11

The various earthy ingredients are included in the second line of the analysis, in this species amounting to 2·05 per cent. One

* Report on Zoophytes, page 713. On page 711, it is suggested by the author that the high degree of hardness, which characterizes corals and also the shells of many molluscs, may arise from the structure of the calcareous secretions being like that of arragonite, instead of common calc-spar. The hardness is near that of arragonite, though sometimes a little exceeding it.

† Op. cit., p. 712, and Silliman's Journal [2], i, 189.

hundred parts of the same, subjected to exact analysis, gave the following result:—

Silica,	22·00
Lime,	13·03
Magnesia,	7·66
Fluorid of calcium,	7·83
Fluorid of magnesium,	12·48
Phosphate of magnesia,	2·70
Alumina (and iron),	16·00
Oxyd of iron,	18·30

In other analyses similar results were obtained, with sometimes a larger proportion of fluorids.

The horny corals, (axes of Gorgoniæ and Antipathi,) were found by Hatchett to have nearly the constitution of ordinary horn.*

The sea-water and the ordinary food of the polyps are evidently the source from which the ingredients of coral are obtained. As coral is an animal secretion, there is no good reason for the surprise with which this subject is sometimes approached. The same powers of elaboration which exist in other animals belong to polyps; for this function, as we have remarked, is the lowest attribute of vitality.

Neither is it at all necessary to inquire whether the lime in sea-water exists as carbonate or sulphate, or whether chlorid of calcium takes the place of these. The powers of life may make from the elements present whatever results the functions of the animal require.†

Various waters were collected in the vicinity of the coral islands, and at different distances from them, for the purpose of analysis in order to compare the constitution of the sea in different parts; but they were lost with the Peacock on the bar of the Columbia river. The proportion of lime salts which occurs in the water of the ocean is about $\frac{1}{30}$ to $\frac{1}{35}$ of all the ingredients in solution. Prof. Forchhammer has ascertained that around the West Indian seas, where corals abound, lime is not as abundant as elsewhere in the ocean, the proportion, according to five analy-

* Report on Zoophytes, p. 56.

† If a drop of sea-water be slowly evaporated under a microscope of high power, crystals of selenite (sulphate of lime) are produced, having the annexed forms, the most common presented by native crystals of this mineral, as stated in works on mineralogy. On adding more water, they are again dissolved; and this may be repeated indefinitely. These results would seem to indicate that the lime was mostly in the state of a sulphate.

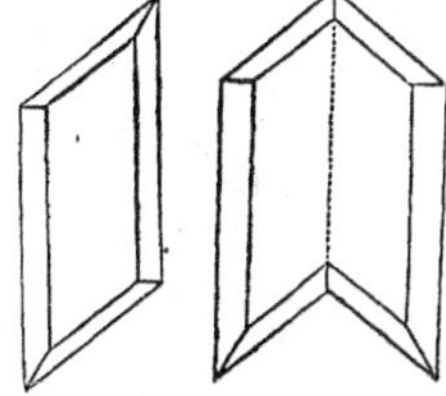

Mr. Darwin states the remarkable fact, described by Mr. Webster, (Voyage of the Chanticleer, ii, 319,) that a deposit of salt and gypsum two feet thick occurs on the shores of Ascension, which was formed by the dash of the waves. Beautiful crystals of selenite were obtained by the writer in logs of half decomposed wood in the shore cliffs near Callao, which were of similar origin.

8

ses, being 247 to 10,000; while in the Kattegat, where the rivers of the Baltic carry it in considerable quantities, the proportion, from four analyses, is 371 to 10,000.* Schweitzer obtained the following result for water taken from the British Channel.†

	Grains.
Water, ...	964·74
Chlorid of sodium, ...	27·06
Chlorid of potassium, . . .	0·77
Chlorid of magnesium, . . .	3·67
Bromid of magnesium, . .	0·03
Sulphate of magnesia, . . .	2·29
Sulphate of lime, . . .	1·41
Carbonate of lime, ...	0·03
	1000·00

Recently, Mr. G. Wilson has detected fluorine in sea-water, showing that all the ingredients of coral are actually contained in the waters of the ocean.‡

It has been common to attribute the origin of the lime of corals to the existence of carbonic acid springs in the vicinity of coral islands. But it is an objection to such a hypothesis, that in the first place the facts do not require it; and in the second, there is no foundation for it. The islands have been supposed to rest on volcanic summits, thus making one hypothesis the basis of another. Carbonic acid springs are by no means a universal attendant on volcanic action. The Pacific affords no one fact in support of such an opinion. There are none on Hawaii, where are the most active fires in Polynesia; and the many explorations of the Society and Navigator Islands have brought none to light. Some of the largest reefs of the Pacific, those of New Holland and New Caledonia, occur where there is no evidence of former volcanic action.§

The currents of the Pacific are constantly bearing new supplies of water over the growing coral beds, and the whole ocean is thus engaged in contributing to their nutriment. Fish, molluscs, and zoophytes are thus provided with earthy ingredients for their calcareous secretions, if their food fails of giving the necessary amount; and by means of the powers of animal life, bones, shells, and corals alike are formed.

The origin of the lime in solution throughout the ocean is an inquiry foreign to our present subject. It is sufficient here to show that this lime, whatever its source, is adequate to explain all the results under consideration.

---

* On Comparative Analytical Researches on Sea-water, by Prof. Forchhammer,—Rep. Brit. Assoc. for 1846, p. 90.

† Lond. and Ed. Phil. Mag. for July, 1839, xv, 51; Amer. Jour. Sci., xxxviii, 12.

‡ Trans. Roy. Soc. of Edinburg, xvi, 145, 1846; Am. Jour. Sci., 2d ser., ii, 114, 1846.

§ See also Darwin, op. cit., p. 60.

3. *Causes influencing the Growth of Coral Zoophytes.*

Marine zoophytes generally require pure ocean water, and they abound especially in the broad inner channels among the reefs, or the large lagoons, and in the shallow waters outside of the breakers. In these channels at the Feejee Group, there are species of every genus, and they grow in the greatest luxuriance, exceeding in profusion and display, all that was elsewhere seen in the Pacific. Here are found the huge Astræa domes, the Meandrinas, Porites, the leafy clusters of the Merulinæ, numerous Madrepores;—indeed nearly all the Pacific corals described in the Report on Zoophytes, exclusive of those from the Tahitian and Hawaiian Islands, were obtained from the inner reefs of the Feejees.* It is therefore an assertion wide from the fact that only smaller corals grow in the lagoons and channels, though true of lagoons and channels of small size, or of such parts of the larger channels as immediately adjoin the mouths of fresh-water streams.

There are undoubtedly species especially fitted for the open ocean; but as peculiar conveniences are required for the collection of zoophytes outside of the line of breakers, we have not the facts necessary for an exact list of such species. From the very abundant masses of Astræas, Meandrinas, Porites, and Madreporas thrown up by the waves on the exposed reefs, it was evident that these genera were well represented in the outer seas. In the Paumotus, the single individuals of Porites lying upon the shores were at times six or eight feet in diameter. Around the Duke of York's Island the bottom was observed to be covered with small branching and foliaceous Madrepores, (Manoporæ,) as delicate as any of the species in more protected waters.

Species of the same genera grow in the face of the breakers, and some are identical with those that occur also in deeper waters. Numerous Astræas, Meandrinas and Madreporas grow at the outer edge of the reefs where the waves come tumbling in with their full force. There are also many Milleporas and some Porites and Pocilloporas in the same places. But the weaker Manoporas, excepting incrusting species, are found in stiller waters either deep or shallow. The Nullipores, properly calcareous vegetation, flourish best along the line of breakers and form thick accumulations upon the reef.†

Again, the same genera occur in the shallow waters of the reef inside of the breakers. Astræas, Meandrinas and Pocil-

* The author's observations on the *species* of corals were not commenced till reaching the Feejees, where we were among the *inner* reefs. Previous to that time, this department in Zoology was in the hands of Mr. J. P. Couthouy.

† Porites and Milleporæ, according to Mr. Darwin, prevail on the surf-reef of Keeling's Island. Chamisso states that the large Astræas live and grow in the breakers.

loporas are not uncommon, though requiring pure waters. There are also Madreporas, some growing even in impure waters. One species was the only coral observed in the lagoon of Honden Island (Paumotus), all others having disappeared owing to its imperfect connection with the sea. Upon the reefs enclosing the harbor of Rewa, (Viti Lebu,) where a large river three hundred yards wide empties, which during freshets enables vessels at anchor two and a half miles off its mouth to dip up fresh water alongside, there is a single porous species of Madrepora, (M. cribripora,) growing here and there in patches over a surface of dead coral rock or sand. In similar places about other regions, species of Porites are most common. In many instances, the living Porites were seen standing six inches above low tide, where they were exposed to sunshine and to rains; and associated with them in such exposed situations, there were usually great numbers of Alcyonia and Xeniæ. Porites also occur in the impure waters adjoining the shores; and the massive species in such places commonly spread out into flat disks, the top dying from the deposition of sediment upon it.

The exposure of six inches above low tide, where the tide is six feet, as in the Feejees, is of much shorter duration than in the Paumotus, where the tide is less than half this amount; and consequently the height of growing coral, as compared with low tide level, varies with the height of the tides. The powers of endurance in some coral zoophytes cannot surprise us, for it is well known that these animals are often very tenacious of life. The hardier species belong mostly to the genera Porites and Pocillopora, besides the family Alcyonidæ.

The small lagoons, when shut out from the influx of the sea, are often rendered too salt for growing zoophytes, in consequence of evaporation,—a condition of the lagoon of Enderby's Island.

Coral zoophytes sometimes suffer injury from being near large fleshy Alcyonia, whose crowded drooping branches lying over against them, destroy the polyps and mar the growing mass. But Serpulas, and certain species of barnacles constituting the genus Criseis, fix themselves upon the living Astræa, Millepora, and other corals, and finally become imbedded by the increase of the zoophyte, without producing any defacement of the surface, or affecting its growth. Many of these Serpulas grow with the same rapidity as the zoophyte, and finally produce a long tube, which penetrates deep within the coral mass; and, when alive, they expand a large and brilliant circle or spiral of delicate rays, making a gorgeous display among the coral polyps. Instinct seems to guide these animals in selecting those corals which correspond with themselves in rate of growth; and there is in general a resemblance between the markings of a Criseis and the character of the radiations of the Astræa it inhabits.

The effects of sediment on growing zoophytes are strongly marked, and may be often perceived when a mingling of fresh water alone produces little influence. We have mentioned that the Porites are reduced to flattened masses by the lodgment of sediment. The same takes place with the hemispheres of Astræa; and it is not uncommon that in this way large areas at top are deprived of life. The other portions still live unaffected by the injury thus sustained. Even the Fungiæ, which are broad simple species, are occasionally destroyed over a part of the disk through the same cause, and yet the rest remains alive. Wherever streams or currents are moving or transporting sediment, there no corals grow; and for the same reason we find no living zoophytes upon sandy or muddy shores.

The influence of *temperature* on the development of animal life, and the distribution of species is well known. But in no department is it more strikingly displayed than in that of zoophytes. In a former report we have considered the general influence of temperature on the several divisions of this order of animals. The remarks which follow are consequently confined to the *reef-forming* species. We reserve for still another page the influence of this cause on the distribution of reefs, since we are occupied here with zoophytes as animal species, and not with reefs, a result from the growth of corals.

The temperature of the ocean in which reef-corals grow is evidently the temperature congenial to them. From a general survey of facts, it appears that these species are not met with where the winter temperature remains much time below 66° F., though a temporary reduction to 64°, or perhaps lower, (as the Bermudas,) may sometimes occur. Where the temperature is above this, even in the hottest parts of the torrid zone, coral zoophytes thrive well. An isothermal line, crossing the ocean where this winter-temperature of the sea is experienced, one north of the equator, and another south, bending in its course by divergence or convergence, wherever the marine currents change its position, will include all the growing reefs of the world; and the area of waters may be properly called the *coral-reef seas.* This *limiting* temperature is found near latitude 28°. Under the equator in the Pacific, the waters where warmest, have the temperature 85° F., and in the Atlantic 83° F.; 66° to 85° is therefore not too great a range of temperature for the various reef-forming corals. Particular species, however, have smaller limits; but these limits have not yet been accurately ascertained.*

* The first application of the well-established principle that temperature influences the growth and distribution of corals is claimed by Mr. J. P. Couthouy equally with myself. Any attempt, however, to determine a limiting temperature he disclaims, and in this particular, as well as the conclusions arrived at, our views are very different. The facts and inferences stated in this place, and on a following page, are deduced throughout from my own study and investigation.

The Porites and Pocilloporæ predominate at Oahu, (Sandwich Islands,) and there are but few of the Astræidæ,—a fact which appears to be explained on the ground that the reefs of that island are not far from the *cold* limits of the coral seas: and it is interesting to observe that these same corals are the hardiest under exposure to impure waters. The warmest parts of the ocean are favorable to the growth of Astræas, Meandrinas, and the allied species; and at the same time, these regions abound in Porites and Pocilloporæ, although the proportion of these corals is smaller than at Oahu.

The genera of reef-forming corals which occur out of the coral-reef seas, belong almost exclusively to the Caryophyllia family, and especially to the genera Dendrophyllia, Caryophyllia, Astroides,* Oculina, and Cyathina, some species of which exist in the Norwegian seas. The Gorgonidæ, Alcyonidæ, Hydroidea, and Actinidæ, extend from the equator nearly to the frigid zone. The Bryozoa have an equally wide range.†

The liability of the lagoons, when contracted in size, to become highly heated by the sun, is probably one cause leading to the depopulation of these internal waters. The temperature becomes raised, as in a puddle of standing water elsewhere, and is quite unfitted, therefore, for species accustomed only to the ordinary tropical temperature of the ocean.

Light and *pressure* and probably the amount of air in sea-water, influence the growth of corals, so far as to fix limits to their distribution in *depth*. It is a little remarkable that those families which have a wide geographical range, have also a great range in depth: for Caryophylliæ, Dendrophylliæ, Oculinæ, Gorgonidæ, and Hydroidea, are found even at depths of one or two hundred fathoms; while Madrepores and Astræas, and all the ordinary reef-forming species scarcely exceed a depth of twenty fathoms.

Temperature has little or no influence in determining this range, although it has been so asserted: 66° is not met with under the equator short of 75 or 100 fathoms. The following table gives approximate results for the winter months, from observations on this point by different navigators in the Pacific. It is well known that these averages are varied much in particular regions by currents.

	Latitude.		Depth of 6° Fahrenheit.
N. Latitude.	28°—30′	- -	0—25 fathoms.
	25°	- -	25—30 "
	20°	- -	30—50 "

* The corals of the Astroides closely resemble those of the Astræa, and have been referred to the latter group by many authors. A related species is found on the coast of this country as high up as lat. 42. An Astræa has been reported from Sydney, New South Wales, which, if a true Astræa, (it has not been described or figured,) gives this genus a wider limit than the coral reef seas.

† See farther, Report on Zoophytes, p. 102.

	Latitude.		Depth of 6° Fahrenheit.
	15°	- -	40—60 fathoms.
	10°	- -	50—75 "
	5°	- -	75 "
EQUATOR.	0°	- -	75—100 "
S. Latitude.	5°	- -	50—75 "
	10°	- -	50 "
	15°	- -	50 "
	20°	- -	40 "
	25°	- -	25 "
	28°—30°	- -	Surface.

It appears, therefore, that among the causes limiting the range of corals in depth, light and hydraulic pressure must have great influence. The proportion of atmospheric air present may be another cause. Yet according to Darondeau, the deeper waters contain more atmospheric air and also more carbonic acid,—the difference being as much as $\frac{1}{100}$th the volume of the water.*

Quoy and Gaymard were the first authors who ascertained that reef-forming corals were confined to small depths, contrary to the account of Forster and the early navigators. The mistake of previous voyagers was a natural one, for coral reefs were proved to stand in an unfathomable ocean; yet it was from the first a mere opinion, as the fact of corals growing at such depths had never been ascertained. It is now considered altogether probable that the bottom of the ocean in its deeper parts is mostly without life of any kind. The few Caryophylliæ and other species which are met with in deep waters, have been shown to be sparsely scattered, mostly of small size, and nowhere form accumulations or beds.

The above-mentioned authors, who explored the Pacific in the Uranie under D'Urville,† concluded from their observations that five or six fathoms (30 or 36 feet) limited their downward distribution. Ehrenberg, by his observations on the reefs of the Red Sea, confirmed the observations of Quoy and Gaymard; he concluded that living corals do not occur beyond six fathoms. Mr. Stutchbury, after a visit to some of the Paumotus and Tahiti, remarks that the living clumps do not rise from a greater depth than 16 or 17 fathoms.‡ Mr. Darwin, who traversed the Pacific with Captain Fitzroy, R. N., gives 20 fathoms as not too great a range, and mentions reported instances of growing reefs in 25 or even 30 fathoms. He states that in the Red Sea, according to Captain Morehead, living corals occur at 25 fathoms. At Keeling Atoll, growing corals are described by him as wholly disap-

* Examination of Sea Water collected during the Voyage of the Bonite, Jameson's Edinb. Jour., July, 1838, p. 164. Darondeau's observations require confirmation.

† Afterwards also in the Astrolabe.

‡ S. Stutchbury, West of England Journal, i, 48.

pearing beyond 20 fathoms; and at the Maldives and Chagos, at a less depth. Other facts brought forward by Mr. Darwin, relate to Caryophylliæ and those species which have a wide range beyond reef-forming zoophytes.

It thus appears that all recent investigators since Quoy and Gaymard have agreed in assigning a comparatively small depth to growing corals. The observations on this point, made during the cruise of the Expedition, tend to confirm this opinion. The conclusion is borne out by the fact that soundings in the course of the various and extensive surveys afford no evidence of growing coral beyond twenty fathoms. Where the depth was fifteen fathoms, coral sand and fragments were almost uniformly reported. Among the Feejee Islands, the extent of coral reef-grounds surveyed was many hundreds of square miles, besides the more careful examination of harbors. The reefs of the Navigator Islands were also sounded out, with others at the Society Group, besides numerous coral islands; and through all these regions no evidence was obtained of corals living at a greater depth than 15 or 20 fathoms. Within the reefs west of Viti Lebu and Vanua Lebu, the anchor of the Peacock was dropped sixty times in water from 12 to 24 fathoms deep, and in no case struck among growing corals; it usually sunk into a muddy or sandy bottom. Patches of reef were encountered at times, but they were at a less depth than 12 fathoms. By means of a drag, occasionally dropped in the same channels, some fleshy Alcyonia, and a few Hydroidea were brought up, but no reef-forming species.

Outside of the reef of Upolu, corals were seen by the writer growing in twelve fathoms. Lieutenant Emmons brought up with a boat-anchor a large Dendrophyllia from a depth of fourteen and a half fathoms at the Feejees; and this species was afterwards found near the surface. Dendrophyllia, it may be remembered, is one of the deep water genera.

These facts, it may be said, are only negative, as the sounding-lead, especially in the manner it is thrown in surveys, would fail of giving decisive results. The character of a growing coral bed is so strongly marked in its uneven surface, its deep holes and many entangling stems, to the vexation of the surveyor, that in general the danger of mistake is small. But allowing uncertainty as great as supposed, there can be little doubt after so numerous observations over so extended regions of reefs.

The depth of the water in harbors and about shores where there is no coral, confirms the view here presented. At Upolu, the depth of the harbors varies generally from twelve to twenty fathoms. On the south side of this island, Lieutenant Perry, off Falealili, one hundred yards from the rocky shores, found bare rocks in eighteen and nineteen fathoms, with no evidence of coral. There is no cause here which will explain the absence of coral, except the depth of water; for corals and coral reefs abound on most other parts of Upolu. Below Falelatai, of the same island, an equal depth was found, with no coral. Off the east cape of Falifa harbor, on the north side of Upolu, Lieutenant Emmons found no coral, although the depth was but eighteen fathoms. About the outer capes of Fungasar harbor, Tutuila, there was no coral, with a depth of fifteen to twenty fathoms; and a line of soundings across from cape to cape, afforded a bottom of sand and shells, in fifteen to twenty-one and a half fathoms. About the capes of Oafonu harbor, on the same island, there was no coral, with a depth of fifteen fathoms.

Similar results were obtained about all the islands surveyed, as the charts satisfactorily show. There is hence little room to doubt that twenty fathoms may be received as near the range in depth for reef corals; and probably the limit lies between fifteen and twenty fathoms, or not far from one hundred feet.

It may be here remarked, that soundings with reference to this subject are liable to be incorrectly reported, by persons who have not particularly studied living zoophytes. It is of the utmost importance, in order that an observation supposed to prove the occurrence of living coral should be of any value, that it be unequivocally determined whether the fragments which a lead may bring up are alive or not when broken off; for a dead fragment proves nothing. Even a strong impression upon the lead, showing the form and character of the surface-cells of a coral, is not wholly satisfactory, as it may have been given by a mass not living. A living fragment, placed in water, will be seen to have a fleshy surface, even if the polyps do not expand. The best observations with reference to this subject would be made with a diving bell.

Much yet remains for farther investigation. Prof. Edward Forbes, in his Zoological Explorations of the Ægean, distinguished three separate regions of invertebrate species within twenty fathoms of the surface: the *first*, or littoral, extending to two fathoms in depth; the *second* from two to ten fathoms; the *third* from ten to twenty fathoms.* Similar subdivisions, or others on the same general principle, may yet be detected in the Pacific, indicated perhaps by zoophytes as well as molluscs. There is no evidence, however, that there are successive beds, composed of a distinct set of species, as has been sometimes suggested. The upraised reefs of Metia afford no proofs of such a mode of formation; on the contrary, they show that the process is continuous and uniform in character through the reef-growing depths. The species in the lower part of the sixteen fathoms are probably different from many of those above; but they pertain to the same gen-

* On the Ægean Invertebrata, E. Forbes, Rep. Brit. Assoc. for 1843, p. 154.

era in most instances, and moreover there are no abrupt transitions; consequently the resulting reefs should have a nearly uniform character, as here stated. This fact may be better appreciated after perusing the following chapter.

The Nullipore zone along the reef-line between low and high tide, is clearly made out by Mr. Darwin, and is one of the interesting results of his investigations. It performs a very important part, by the protection it gives the reef from abrasion. The exposed reef is thus gathering lime from the waters, and extending itself, when, if devoid of this protection, it would be constantly yielding to the sea. On the inner reefs where the protection is not needed, it is not given; some species of Nullipore, however, occur in these regions, and others are found at various depths.

As the Caryophyllia family extend into deeper waters than most other reef-corals, it might be inferred that these at least may constitute a lower bed, or substratum. But this is by no means the case. As just stated, one species (the Dendrophyllia nigrescens) was found at 14½ fathoms and also of identical characters at low tide level. The Caryophylliæ are but sparingly distributed; the species are few, and mostly small; and not a dozen different kinds were detected in the Pacific. Their contributions to reefs are therefore inconsiderable.

4. *Rate of Growth of Zoophytes.*

The rate of growth of zoophytes, is a subject but little understood. We do not refer here to the progress of a reef in formation, which is another question complicated by many co-operating causes; but simply to the rapidity with which particular species of coral-zoophytes increase in size. There is no doubt that the rate is different for different species. It is moreover probable that it corresponds with the rate of growth of other allied polyps that do not secrete lime. The rate of growth of Actiniæ might give us an approximation to the rate of growth in a Mussa, which are coral animals of like size and general characters; for the additional function of secreting lime, would not retard necessarily the maturing of the polyp; and from the rate of growth of the same animals in the young state, we might perhaps draw some inferences as to the rate in polyps of corresponding size. But no observations on this point were made by us while abroad.

Although the rapidity is undoubtedly far less than was formerly reported, the following facts from different sources seem to show that the rate is still greater than has been of late believed. Mr. Darwin, citing from a manuscript by Dr. Allen of Forres, some experiments made on the east coast of Madagascar, states that, in December, 1830, twenty corals were placed by this gentleman apart on a sandbank, in three feet water, (low tide,) and in the July following, each had nearly reached the surface, and was quite immovable; and some had grown over the others. Mr. Stutchbury describes a specimen consisting of a species of oyster, whose age could not be over two years, encrusted by an Agaricia, weighing two pounds nine ounces.* It is stated by M. Duchassaing, in a letter from Guadeloupe, that in two months, some large individuals of the *Madrepora prolifera*, which he broke away, were restored to their original size.†

Since the return of the Expedition, I have received a letter containing some facts on the growth of Actiniæ from Sir J. G. Dalyell, whose able observations in this department of science are highly curious and important. After speaking of the various conditions and sizes of the young at birth, and of the difference in the rapidity of growth depending on the amount of nutriment at hand, he says, speaking of a Scottish species of Actinia, "The dimensions will generally double in a fortnight from its birth. The diameter of the base being originally about an eighth of an inch, or hardly as much, will be five-eighths in six months, and the tentacles will occupy a circle of an inch and a half in diameter. In twelve or thirteen months, the diameter of the base will reach an inch and the expansion of the tentacles two inches between the tips. An Actinia whose tentacula expanded a quarter of an inch three weeks after it was produced, enlarged so much in five months that they expanded an inch, and the body was then half an inch thick." If we reason upon these data, and assume that the Madrepore polyps may increase lineally in six months as much as the young Actinia, we shall have an elongation of five-eighths or three-fourths of an inch in six months. Taking the still more rapid rate, of doubling in a fortnight, which might be more correct, since the Madrepore polyps are about the size of the Actinia in its earliest state, we should have a lengthening of a fourth of an inch in a month, and three inches a year. The data upon which this conclusion is based, though important, are uncertain, but would probably give too high rather than too low an estimate. And yet it is far below the rate apparently established by the experiments with corals cited in the preceding paragraph. We must admit that the subject requires more accurate investigation.

The stay of the expedition near any particular reef in the Pacific was too short for any examinations by us. They might easily be made by those residing in coral seas, either in the manner adopted by Mr. Allan, or more definitely by placing marks upon particular species. By inserting slender glass pins a certain distance from the summit of a Madrepore, its growth might be

* West of England Journal, vol. i, p. 50,

† L'Institut, No. 639, April 1, 1846, p. 111.

accurately measured from month to month. Two such pins in the surface of an Astræa, would in the same manner, by the enlarging distance between, show the rate of increase in the circumference of the hemisphere; or if four were placed so as to enclose an area, and the number of polyps counted, the numerical increase of polyps resulting from budding, might be ascertained. It is to be hoped that some of the foreign residents at the Sandwich, Society, Samoan or Feejee Islands will take this subject in hand. There are also many parts of the West Indies, where these investigations might be conveniently made.

CHAPTER III.

FORMATION OF REEFS, AND CAUSES OF THEIR FEATURES AND GEOGRAPHICAL DISTRIBUTION.

An inquiry into the causes and origin of the features presented by coral reefs and islands, has led us to glance at the nature of coral zoophytes, and at the effects of various agents upon their development. The way has thus been prepared for considering the bearing of these facts, and of other influencing causes, on the growth of the coral plantation as a whole. While, therefore, the preceding pages treat of zoophytes as individual species, the following will relate to those results which proceed from their accumulation, and the causes which have determined the features and geographical distribution of reefs and islands.

1. *Formation of Reefs.*

Very erroneous ideas prevail, respecting the appearance of a bed or area of growing corals. The submerged reef is often thought of as an extended mass of coral, alive uniformly over its upper surface, and, by this living growth, gradually enlarging upward: and such preconceived views, when ascertained to be erroneous by observation, have sometimes led to skepticism with regard to the zoophytic origin of the reef-rock. Nothing is wider from the truth: and this must have been inferred from the descriptions already given. Another glance at the coral plantation should be taken by the reader, before proceeding with the explanations which follow.

Coral plantation and coral field, are more appropriate appellations than coral garden, and convey a juster impression of the surface of a growing reef. Like a spot of wild land, covered in some parts with varied shrubbery, in other parts bearing only occasional tufts of vegetation over barren plains of sand, here a clump of saplings, and there a carpet of variously colored flowers —such is the coral plantation. Numerous kinds of zoophytes grow scattered over the surface, like vegetation upon the land: there are large areas that bear nothing, and others that are thickly overgrown. There is, however, no green sward to the landscape; sand and fragments fill up the bare intervals between the flowering tufts: or where the zoophytes are crowded, there are deep holes among the stony stems and folia.

These observations will prepare the mind for some disappointment in a first view of coral reefs. Nature does not make greenhouses, but distributes widely her beauties, and leaves it for man to gather into gardens the choicer varieties. Yet there are scenes in the coral landscape, which justify the brightest coloring of the poet: where coral shrubbery and living flowers are mingled in profusion; where Astræa domes appear like the gemmed temples of the coral world, and Madrepore vases, the decorations of the groves; and as the forests and flowers of land have their birds and butterflies, so

> "——— Life in rare and beautiful forms
> Is sporting amid those bowers of stone,"

for fish of various hues, red, blue, purple, green, and other brilliant shades, keep constant play, appearing and disappearing among the branches.

These fields of growing coral spread over submarine lands, such as the shores of islands and continents, where the depth is not greater than their habits require, just as vegetation extends itself through regions that are congenial. The germ or ovule, which, when first produced, swims free, finds afterwards a point of rock or dead coral to plant itself upon, and thence springs the tree, or some other form of coral growth.

The analogy to vegetation does not stop here. It is well known that the debris of the forest, decaying leaves and stems, and animal remains, add to the soil; and that accumulations of this kind are ceaselessly in progress: that by this means, in the luxuriant swamp, deep beds of peaty earth are formed. So it is in the coral mead. Accumulations of fragments and sand from the coral zoophytes, and of shells and other relics of organic life, are in constant progress; and thus a bed of coral debris is formed and compacted. There is this difference, that a large part of the vegetable material consists of elements which escape as gases on decomposition, whereas coral is itself an enduring rock-material undergoing no change except the mechanical one of comminution. The animal portion is but a mere fraction of the whole zoophyte.

In these few hints, we have the whole theory of reef-making: not a speculative opinion, but a legitimate deduction from a few simple facts, and bearing close analogy to operations on land. The coral debris and shells fill up the intervals between the coral patches, and the cavities among the living tufts, and in this manner produce the reef deposit, which is finally consolidated while still beneath the water.

The coral-zoophyte is especially adapted for such a mode of reef accumulation. Were the nourishment drawn from below, as in most plants, the solidifying coral rock would soon destroy all life: instead of this, the tree is gradually dying below while growing above; and the accumulations cover only the dead portions. Moreover, to prevent accident, where these accumulations do not keep pace with the progress of death, organic incrustations cover the lifeless trunk, and protect it from the dissolving waters.

But on land, there is the decay of the year and that of old age producing vegetable debris; and storms prostrate forests. And are there corresponding effects among the groves of the sea? It has been shown that coral plantations, from which reefs proceed, do not grow in the "calm and still" depths of the ocean. They are to be found amid the very waves, and extend but little below a hundred feet, which is far within the reach of the sea's heavier commotions.* Here is an agent which is not without its effects. The enormous masses of uptorn rock found on many of the islands may give some idea of the force of the lifting wave; and there are examples on record, to be found in various Treatises on Geology, of still more surprising effects.†

---

* During the more violent gales, the bottom of the sea is said, by different authors, to be disturbed to a depth of three hundred, three hundred and fifty, or even five hundred feet, and De la Beche remarks, that when the depth is fifteen fathoms, the water is very evidently discolored by the action of the waves on the sand and mud of the bottom. In the *Comptes Rendus*, t. xii, 774, M. Siau mentions that parallel ridges are formed on the bottom, by the motion of the water, which may be readily distinguished at a depth of at least twenty meters. The hollows between such ridges or zones are occupied by the heavier substances of the bottom. Similar zones were distinguished at a depth of one hundred and eighty-eight meters, to the Northwest of the St. Paul's Roads.

† Lyell, vol. ii, p. 38–40. Speaking of the force of waves on coasts, Lyell mentions the transportation of a block of stone, ninety feet from its bed, which was eight feet two inches, by seven feet, and five feet one inch in its dimensions, and another nine feet two inches, by six and a half feet, by four feet, having been "hurried up an acclivity to a distance of one hundred and fifty feet."

In an article on the subject, by Thomas Stevenson, of Edinburgh, published in the Transactions of the Royal Society of Edinburgh, (vol. xvi, 1845,) it is stated, as a deduction from two hundred and sixty-seven experiments, extending over twenty-three successive months, that the average force for Skerryvore, for five of the summer months, during the years 1843, 1844, was six hundred and eleven pounds per square foot; and for six of the winter months of the same year, it was two thousand and eighty-six pounds per square foot, or three times as great as during the summer months. During a westerly gale, at the same place, in March, 1845, a pressure of six thousand and eighty-three pounds was registered by Mr. Stevenson's dynamometer, (the name of the instrument used.) He mentions several remarkable instances of transported blocks. One of gneiss, containing five hundred and four cubic feet, was carried by the waves five feet from the place where it lay, and there became wedged so as no longer to the moved. Of the manner in which it was moved, Mr. Reid (as cited by Mr. Stevenson) says: "The sea, when I saw it striking the stone, would wholly immerse or bury it out of sight, and the run extended up to the grass line above it, making a perpendicular rise of from thirty-nine to forty feet above high water level. On the incoming waves striking the stone, we could see this monstrous mass, of upwards of forty tons weight, lean landwards, and the back-run would uplift it again with a jerk, leaving it with very little water about it, when the next incoming wave made it recline again."

Mr. Stevenson states also that the Bell Rock Lighthouse in the German Ocean, though one hundred and twelve feet in height, is literally buried in foam and spray, to the very top, during ground swells, when there is no wind. On the 20th of November, 1827, the spray rose to the height of one hundred and seventeen feet above the foundations or low water mark; and deducting eleven feet for the tide that day, it leaves one hundred and six feet, which is equivalent to a pressure of *nearly three tons per square foot.*

With such facts, any incredulity respecting the power of waves should be laid aside. Moreover, it may be remarked that the Pacific is a much wider ocean than the Atlantic, with far heavier waves in its ordinary state.

We must, therefore, allow that some effect will be produced upon the coral groves. There will be trees prostrated by gales, as on land, fragments scattered, and fragmentary and sand accumulations commenced. Besides, masses of the heavier corals will be uptorn, and carried along over the coral plantation, which will destroy and grind down everything in their way. So many are the accidents of this kind to which zoophytes appear to be exposed, that we might believe they would often be exterminated, were they not singularly tenacious of life, and ready to sprout anew on any rock where they may find quiet long enough to give themselves again a firm attachment.

But it should be observed, that the sea would have far less effect upon the slender forms characterizing many zoophytes, among which the water finds free passage, than on the massive rock, against whose sides a large volume may drive unbroken. Moreover, much the greater part of the strength of the ocean is exerted near tide level, where it rises in breakers which plunge against the shores. Yet, owing to the many nooks and recesses deep among the corals, the rapidly moving waters, during the heavier swells, must produce whirling eddies of considerable force, tending to uproot or break the coral clumps. These disrupting and transporting effects, will be less and less as we recede from the shores; yet all coral depths must experience them in some degree.

There is another process going on over the coral field, somewhat analogous to vegetable decay, though still very different. Zoophytes have been described as ever dying while living. The dead portions have the surface much smoothed, or deprived of the roughening points which belong to the living coral, and the cells are sometimes half obliterated, or the delicate lamellæ worn away. This may be viewed as one source of fine coral particles; and as the process is constantly going on, it is not altogether unimportant. This material is in a fit condition to enter into solution, and it cannot be doubted that the water receives lime from this source, which is afterwards yielded to the reef.

In the Alcyonia family, which includes semi-fleshy corals, and the Gorgoniæ, the lime is often scattered through the polyps in granules; and the process of death sets these calcareous grains free, which are consequently added to the coral sands. The same process has been supposed to take place in the more common reef corals, the Madrepores and Astræas, and it is possible that this may be to some extent the case. Yet it would seem, from facts observed, that after the secretion has begun within the polyp, the secretion of lime going on takes place *against* the portions already formed and in direct union with them, and not as granules to be afterwards cemented.

The *mud-like* deposits about coral reefs have been attributed to the causes just mentioned, but without due consideration. There is an unfailing and abundant source of this kind of material in the self-triturating sands of the reefs acted upon by the moving waters. On the seaward side of the coral island, and on the shores of the larger lagoons, where the surface rises into waves of much magnitude, the finer portions are carried off, and the coarser sand remains alone to form the beaches. This is a well known fact common on all shores exposed to the waves, coral or not coral, and to this cause the sandy character is attributed. But in the smaller lagoons, where the water is only rippled by the winds, or roughened for short intervals, the trituration is of the gentlest kind possible, and, moreover, the finely pulverized material remains as part of the shores. Thus the fine material of the mud must be constantly forming on all the shores, for the sands are perpetually wearing themselves out; but the mud *accumulates* only in the more quiet waters, and within the lagoons and channels, where it settles, after being washed out from the beaches. This corresponds exactly with the facts; and every lake pool or water of our continents illustrates the same point.*

The coral world, as we thus perceive, is planted like the land with a variety of shrubs and smaller plants, and the elements and natural decay are producing gradual accumulations of material, like those of vegetation. The history of the growing reef has consequently its counterpart among the ordinary occurrences of the land about us.

The progress of the coral formation is like its commencement. The same causes continue with similar results, and the reader might easily supply the details from the facts already presented. The production of debris will necessarily continue to go on: a part will be swept by the waves, across the patch of reef, into

---

* Mr. Darwin, in discussing the origin of the finer calcareous mud, (op. cit., p. 14,) supposes that it is derived, in part, from Fishes and Holothurias, and other authors have thrown out the same suggestion. He cites as a fact, on the authority of Mr. Liesk, that certain fish browse on the living zoophytes; and from Mr. Allan, of Forres, he learned also that Holothurias subsisted on them. With regard to the facts here stated, I can make no definite assertion. Small fish swarm about the branching clumps, and when disturbed, seek shelter at once among the branches, where they are safe from pursuit: I have often witnessed this fact, and never saw reason to suppose that they clustered about the coral for any other purpose. It is an undoubted fact, however, as stated by Mr. Darwin, that fragments of coral and sand may be found in the stomachs of these animals, though this is not sufficient evidence of their browsing on the coral. The conclusion deduced by him from the facts may be justly doubted. The fish and Holothurias, though numerous, are quite inadequate for the supply; and, moreover, we have, as explained above, an abundant source of the finest coral material without such aid. Motion of particle over particle, will necessarily wear to dust, even though the particles be diamonds; and this incessant grinding action about reefs, accounts satisfactorily for the deposits of coral mud, however great their extent.

the lagoon or channel beyond, while other portions lodge on its surface. But besides the small fragments, larger masses will be thrown on the reefs, by the more violent waves, and commence to raise them above the sea. The *clinker fields* of coral, by this means produced, constitute the first step in the formation of dry land. Afterwards, by farther contributions of the coarse and fine coral material, the islets are completed, and raised as far out of water as the waves can reach—that is, from six to ten feet. The Ocean is thus the architect, while the coral polyps afford the material for the structure: and when all is ready, it sows the land with seed brought from distant shores, covering it with verdure and flowers.

The growth of the reefs and islands around high lands, is the same as here described for the atoll. The reef rock in all cases is mainly a result of accumulations of coral and shell debris. There are reefs where the corals retain the position of growth, as has been described on a former page. But with these, the debris comes in to fill up the intervening spaces or cavities, and make a compact bed for consolidation. There are other parts, especially the outer reef along the line of breakers, which are formed by the gradual growth of layer upon layer of incrusting Nullipores; but in the Pacific, such formations are of small extent.*

Among the peculiarities of coral islands, the *shore platform* appears to be one of the most singular. It will be remembered that it lies but little above low tide level, and is often three hundred feet in width, with a nearly flat surface throughout.

Though apparently so peculiar, the existence of this platform is due to the simple action of the sea, and is a necessary result of this action. Passing to New Holland, from the coral islands of the tropics, we there found the same structure exemplified along the *sandstone* shores of this semi-continent, where it is continued for scores of miles. At the base of the sandstone cliff, in most places one or more hundred feet in height, there is a layer of sandstone rock, lying, like the shore platform of the coral island, near low tide level, and from fifty to one hundred and fifty yards in width. It is continuous with the bottom layer of the cliff: the rocks which once covered it, have been removed by the sea. Its outer edge is the surf-line of the shore. At low tide it is mostly a naked flat of rock, while at high tide it is wholly under water, and the sea reaches the cliff. New Zealand, at the Bay of Islands, afforded us the same fact, again, in an argillaceous sand-rock; and there was no stratification in this case to favor the production of a horizontal surface; it was a direct result from the

* Prof. Agassiz has recently observed that deposits of this last kind constitute in many places the reef rock about the Florida Keys.

causes at work. The shore shelf stands about five feet above low water. A small island in this bay is well named the "Old

"THE OLD HAT," BAY OF ISLANDS.

Hat," the platform encircling it, as shown in the above figure, forming a broad brim to a rude conical crown. The water, in these cases, has worn away the cliffs, leaving the basement untouched.

A surging wave, as it comes upon a coast, gradually rears itself on the shallowing shores; finally, the waters at top, through their greater velocity, plunge with violence upon the barrier before it. The force of the ocean's surges is therefore mostly confined to their summit waters, which add weight to superior velocity, and drive violently upon whatever obstacle is presented. The *lower* waters of the surge advance steadily but more slowly, owing to the retarding friction of the bottom; the motion they have is directly forward, and thus they act with little mechanical advantage; moreover, they gradually swell over the shores, and receive, in part, the force of the *upper* waters. The wave, after breaking, sweeps up the shore till it gradually dies away. Degradation from this source is consequently most active where the upper or plunging portion of the breaker strikes.

But, further, we observe that at low tide the sea is comparatively quiet; it is during the influx and efflux that the surges are heaviest. The action commences after the rise, is strongest from half to three-fourths tide, and then diminishes again near high tide. Moreover, the plunging part of the wave is raised considerably above the general level of the water. From these considerations, it is apparent that the line of greatest wave-action, must be above low water level. Let us suppose a tide of three feet, in which the action would probably be strongest when the tide had risen two feet out of the three; and let the height of the advancing surge be four feet:—the wave, at the time of striking, would stand, with its summit, three feet above high tide level; and from this height would plunge obliquely downward against the rock, or any obstacle before it. It is obvious, that under such circumstances, the greatest force would be felt, not far from the line of high tide, or between that line and three feet above it. In regions where the tide is higher than just supposed, as six feet for example, the same height of wave would give nearly the same height to the line of wave action, as compared with high tide level. Under the influence of heavier waves, such as are common during storms, the line of wave-action would be at a still higher elevation, as may be readily estimated by the reader.

Besides a line of the *greatest* wave-action, we may also distinguish a height where this action is entirely null; and it is evident, from facts already stated, that the point will be found somewhat above low tide level. The lower waters of the surge, instead of causing degradation, are *accumulative* in their ordinary action, when the material exposed to them is movable: they are constantly piling up, while the upper waters are rending and preparing material to be carried off. The height at which these two operations balance one another will be the height, therefore, of the line of no degradation. As the sea at low tide is mostly quiet, and the lower of the surging waters swell on to receive the upper and parry the blow, and moreover, there is next a return current outward,—we should infer that the line would be situated more or less above low tide, according to the height of the tide, and the surges accompanying it. We are not left to conjecture on this point; for the examples presented by the shores of New Holland and New Zealand afford definite facts. Degradation has there taken place sufficient to carry off cliffs of rock, of great extent; yet below a certain level, the sea has had little or no effect. This height, at New Holland, is three feet above ordinary low tide, and at New Zealand, about five feet. With regard to the height varying with the tides, we observe that in the Paumotus, where the water rises but two or three feet, the platform is seldom over four to six inches above low tide, which is proportionally less than at New Holland and New Zealand, where the tide is six and eight feet. From these observations, it appears that the height of *no wave-action*, as regards the degradation of a coast under ordinary seas, is situated near one-fifth tide, in the Paumotus, and above half tide at New Zealand, showing a great difference between the effect of the comparatively quiet surges of the middle Pacific, and the more violent of New Zealand. Within the Bay of Islands, where the sea has not its full force, the platform, as around the "Old Hat," is but little above low water level. The exact relation of the height of the platform to the height and force of the tides remains to be determined more accurately by observation. While, therefore, the height of the shore platform depends on the tides, and the usual strength of the waves, the breadth of it will be determined by the same causes in connection with the nature of the rock-material.*

* On basaltic shores it is not usual to find a shore platform, as the rock scarcely undergoes any degradation, except from the most violent seas; such coasts are con-

It is apparent that one single principle meets all the various cases. The rocky platform of some sea-shores, the low tide sand-spit on others, and the coral-reef platform of others, require but one explanation. The material of the coral platform is piled up by the advancing surges, and cemented through the infiltrating waters. These surges, advancing towards the edge of the shelf, swell over it before breaking, and thus throw a protection about the exposed rocks; and as the tide rises, this protection is complete. They move on, sweeping over the shelf, but only clear it of sand and fragments, which they bear to the beach.

The isolated blocks in the Paumotus which stand on the platform, attached to it below, are generally most worn one or two feet above high tide level, a fact which corresponds with the statement in a preceding paragraph with regard to the height of the greatest wave-action.

In addition to this ordinary wave-action, there are also more violent effects from storms; and these are observed alike on the Australian shores referred to, and on those of coral islands. The waters, moving through greater depths, and driving on with increased velocity up the shallowing shores among cavities or under shelving layers, break and lift the rocks of the edge of the platform, and throw them on the reef. From the observations of Mr. Stevenson, cited in a note to a preceding page, it appears that the force of the waves during the summer and winter months differs at Skerryvore more than 1200 pounds to the square foot, —in the former it averaging but 636 pounds, and in the latter 2086 pounds, while in storms it was at times equivalent to 6083 pounds. The seasons are not as unlike in the tropical part of the Pacific. Still there must be a marked difference between the ordinary seas and those during stormy weather. We have therefore no difficulty in comprehending how the ordinary wave-action should build up and keep entire the shore platform, while the more agitated seas may tear up parts of the structure formed, and bear them on to the higher parts of the island. Still more violent in action are the great earthquake-waves, which move through the very depths of the ocean.

These principles offer an explanation also of the general fact that the windward reef is the highest. The ordinary seas, both on the leeward and windward sides, are sufficient for producing coral debris and building up the reef, and in this work the two sides may go on with almost equal rate of progress: consequently we may often find no very great difference in the *width* of the

---

sequently often covered with large fragments of the basaltic rocks. But on sand stone shores, this gradual action keeps the platform of nearly uniform breadth. Moreover, any uptorn masses thrown upon it, are soon destroyed by the same action, and carried off; and thus the platform is kept nearly clean of debris, even to the base of the cliff.

leeward and windward reefs, especially as the wind for some parts of the year has a course opposite to its usual direction. But seldom, except on the side to windward, is a sufficient force brought to bear upon the edge of the platform, to detach and uplift the larger coral blocks. The distance to which the waves may roll on without becoming too much weakened for the transportation of uptorn blocks, will determine the outline of the forming land. With proper data as to the force of the waves, the tides, and the soundings around. the extent of the shore platform might be made a subject of calculation.

The effect of a windward reef in diminishing the force of the sea is sometimes shown in the influence of one island on another. A striking instance of this is presented by the northernmost of the Tarawan Islands. All the islands of this group are well wooded to windward—the side fronting east, between north and south. But the north side of Tari-tari is nothing but a bare reef, through a distance of twenty miles, although the southeast reef is a continuous line of verdure. The small island of Makin, just north of Tari-tari, is the breakwater which has protected the reef referred to from the heavier seas.

Coral island accumulations have one advantage over all other shore deposits, owing to the ready agglutination of calcareous grains, as explained on a following page. It has been stated that coral sandrocks are forming along the beaches, while the reef-rock is consolidating in the water. A defence of rock against encroachment is thus produced, and is in continual progress. Moreover, the structure built amid the waves will necessarily have the form and condition best fitted for withstanding their action. The little islet of an atoll is therefore more enduring than hills of harder basaltic rocks. Reefs of zoophytic growth but "mock the leaping billows," while other lands of the same height gradually yield to the assaults of the ocean. There are cases, however, of wear from the sea, owing to some change of condition in the island, or in the currents about it, in consequence of which, parts once built up are again carried off. Moreover, those devastating seas which overleap the whole land may occasion unusual degradation from some parts. Yet these islets have within themselves the source of their own repair, and are secure from all serious injury.

The lagoons in coral islands are constantly receiving more or less debris from the reefs; and patches of growing coral within also tend to fill them up. But the effect is slow in its progress, and none but islands of small size, as before stated, show any approximation to an obliteration of the lagoon.

2. *Causes modifying the Forms and Growth of Reefs.*

Coral reefs although (1) *dependent on the configuration of the submarine lands for many of their features*, undergo various modifications of form or condition through the influence of extraneous causes, such as (2) *unequal exposure to the waves*; (3) *oceanic or local currents*; (4) *presence of fresh or impure waters.* In briefly treating of these topics, we may consider first, reefs around high islands, and afterwards, atoll reefs. The effect of the waves on different sides of reefs has already been considered, and we pass on, therefore, at once to the influence of oceanic or local currents, and fresh or impure waters.

a. Barrier and Fringing Reefs.—The *existence of harbors* about coral-bound lands, and of entrances through reefs, is largely attributable to the action of tidal or local marine currents. The presence of freshwater streams has some effect towards the same end, but much less than has been supposed.*

There are usually strong tidal currents through the reef channels and openings. These currents are modified in character by the outline of the coast, and are strongest wherever there are coves or bays to receive the advancing tides. The harbor of Apia, on the north side of Upolu, affords a striking illustration of this general principle. The coast at this place has an indentation 2000 yards wide and nearly 1000 deep, as in the accompanying sketch, reduced from the chart by the Expedition. The reef extends from either side or cape a mile out to sea, leaving between, an entrance for ships. The harbor averages ten feet in depth, and at the entrance is fifteen feet. In this harbor there is a remarkable out-current along the bottom, which during gales, is so strong at certain states of the tide, that a ship at anchor, although a wind may be blowing directly in the harbor, will often ride with a slack cable; and in more moderate weather the vessel may tail out *against* the wind. Thus when no current but one inward is perceived at the surface, there is an under current acting against the keel and bottom of the vessel, which is of sufficient strength to counteract the influence of the winds on the rigging and hull. The cause of such a current is obvious. The sea is constantly pouring water over the

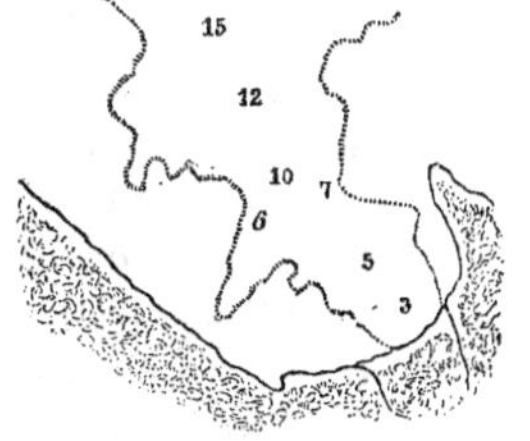

HARBOR OF APIA, UPOLU.

* The view here supported, is nearly identical with that presented by Mr. Darwin, (op. cit., page 68.) The arguments given were, however, written out (in 1840), before his descriptions of coral islands were known to me. This fact may give additional weight to the opinions, inasmuch as they are therefore the conclusions of independent observers, and are substantiated by a distinct set of observations.

reefs into the harbor, and the tides are periodically adding to the accumulation; the indented shores form a narrowing space where these waters tend to pile up: escape consequently takes place along the bottom by the harbor-entrance, this being the only means of exit. This is a correct history of numerous cases about all the islands. In a group like the Feejees, where many of the islands are large, and the reefs very extensive, the currents are still more remarkable, and they change in direction with the tides. The general mode of action, however, is the same.

A current of water of the kind here represented, will carry out much coral debris, and strew it along its course. The transported material will vary in amount from time to time, according to the force and direction of the current. It is therefore evident that the ground over which it runs is wholly unfit for the growth of coral, since zoophytes are readily destroyed by depositions of earth or sand, and require a firm basement to commence growth. The existence of an opening through a reef requires, therefore, no other explanation; and it is obvious that harbors may generally be expected to exist wherever the character of the coast is such as to produce currents and give a fixed direction to them.

The currents about the reef grounds west of the large Feejee Islands, aid in distributing the debris both of the land and the reefs. In some parts, the currents eddy and deposit their detritus; in others they sweep the bottom clean. Thus, under these varying conditions, there may be growing corals over the bottom in some places and not in others; and the reefs may be distributed in patches, when without such an influence we should expect a general continuity of coral reef over the whole reef-grounds.

The results from marine currents are often increased by waters from the island streams; for the coves, where harbors are most likely to be found, are also the embouchures of valleys and the streamlets they contain. The fresh waters poured in add to the amount of water, and increase the rapidity of the out-current. At Apia, Upolu, there is a stream thirty yards wide; and many other similar instances might be mentioned. These waters from the land bring down also much detritus, especially during freshets, and the depositions aid those from marine currents in keeping the bottom clear of growing coral. These are the principal means by which freshwater streams contribute towards determining the existence of harbors; for little is due to their freshening the salt waters of the sea.

The small influence of the last-mentioned cause—the one most commonly appealed to—will be obvious, when we consider the size of the streams of the Pacific islands, and the fact that fresh water is lighter than salt, and therefore, instead of sinking, flows on over its surface. The deepest rivers are seldom over six feet, even at their mouths; and three or four feet is a more usual depth. They will have little effect, therefore, on the sea water beneath this depth, for they cannot sink below it; and corals may consequently grow even in front of a river's mouth. Moreover, the river water becomes mingled with the salt, and, in most cases, a short distance out, would not be unfit for some species of coral zoophytes.

Yet when the rivers are large, like those of continents, the influence of the freshening waters is very decided, and prevails often over a wide extent of coast.

Freshwater streams, acting in all the different modes pointed out, are of little importance in harbor-making about the islands of the Pacific. The harbors, with scarcely an exception, would have existed without them. They tend, however, by the detritus they deposit, to keep the bottom more free from growing patches of coral, and consequently produce better anchorage ground: moreover, within the harbors they usually keep channels open through or over the shore reef sufficiently deep and wide for a boat to reach the land, and sometimes preserve a clean sand-beach throughout. That this is their principal effect will appear from a few facts.

The figure on page 14, has been described as a map of the reef of North Tahiti, between Papieti on the left, and Venus Point on the right.

a. The harbor of Papieti is enclosed by a reef about three-fourths of a mile from the shore. The entrance through the reef is narrow, with a depth of eleven fathoms at center, six to seven fathoms either side, and three to five close to the reef. This fine harbor receives an unimportant streamlet, while a much larger stream empties just to the east of the east cape, *opposite which the reef is close at hand and unbroken.*

b. Toanoa is the harbor next east of Papieti. The entrance is thirty-five fathoms deep at middle, and three and a half to five fathoms near the points of reef. There is no freshwater stream, excepting a trifling rivulet.

c. Papaoa is an open expanse of water, harbor-like in character, but is without any entrance; the reef is unbroken. Yet there are two streams emptying into it, one of which is of considerable size.

d. Off Matavai, the place next east, the reef is interrupted for about two miles. The harbor is formed by an extension of the reef off Point Venus, the east cape. There is no stream on the coast, opposite this interruption in the reef, except towards Point Venus, and at the present time the waters find their principal exit, east of the Point, behind a large coral reef, but a quarter of a mile distant.

From such facts, it is evident that the growth of coral reefs is not much retarded by freshwater streams. We cannot be surprised at the little influence they appear to have exerted when knowing that none of these so-called rivers are over three feet in depth; and the most that they can do is to produce a thin layer of brackish water over the sea within the channels.

e. The annexed figure of the harbor of Falifa, Upolu, represents another coral harbor, as surveyed by Lieutenant Emmons. At its head there is a fine stream twenty-five or thirty yards wide, and three feet deep. Notwithstanding the unusual size of the river, the coral reef lies near its mouth, and projects some distance in front of it. Its surface is dead, but corals are growing upon its outer slope.

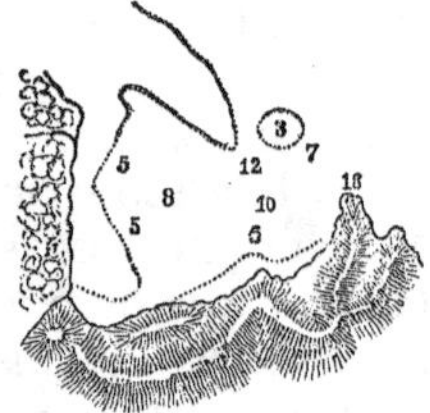
HARBOR OF FALIFA.

f. The harbor of Rewa, in the Feejees, may be again alluded to. The waters received by the bay amount to at least 500,000 cubic feet a minute. Yet there is an extensive reef enclosing the bay, lying but three miles from the shores, and with only two narrow openings for ships. The case is so remarkable that we can hardly account for the facts without supposing the river's mouth to have neared the reef by depositions of detritus since the inner parts of the reef were formed; and there is some evidence that this was the case, though to what distance, we cannot definitely state. With this admission, the facts may still surprise us; yet they are explained on the principle that fresh water does not sink in the ocean, but is superficial, and runs on in a distinct channel; its effect is almost wholly through hydrostatic pressure, and detritus depositions. Besides these instances, there are many others in the Feejees, as will be observed on the Expedition charts. Mokungai has a large harbor, without a stream of fresh water;—so also Vakea, and Direction Island.

The instances brought forward are a fair example of what is to be found throughout coral seas; and they establish, beyond dispute, that while much in harbor-making should be attributed to the transported sand or earth of marine and freshwater currents, in preventing the growth of coral, but little is due to the freshening influence of the streams of the islands.

But while observing that currents have so decided an influence on the condition of harbors, we should remember another prevalent cause, already remarked upon, and perhaps more wide in its effects than those just considered. I refer to the features of the supporting land, or the character of soundings off a coast. We need not repeat here what has already been dwelt upon, showing that many of the interruptions of reefs have thus arisen. The wide break off Matavai may be of this kind. The widening of the inner channel at Papieti, forming a space for a harbor, may be another example of it; for the reef here extends to a greater distance from the shores, as if because the waters shallowed more gradually outward off this part of the coast. The same cause—the depth of soundings, on the principle that corals do not grow where the depth much exceeds a hundred feet—has more or less influence about all reefs in determining their configuration and the outlines of harbors. A remarkable instance of the latter is exemplified in the annexed chart of Whippey harbor, Viti Lebu, reduced from the chart of the Expedition to the scale of half an inch to the mile.

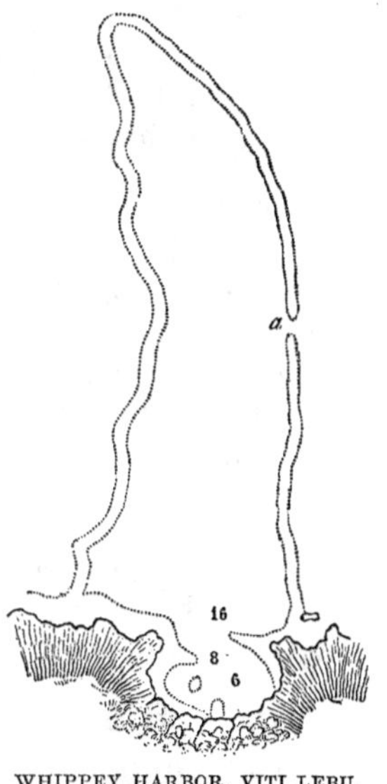

WHIPPEY HARBOR, VITI LEBU.

The existence of harbors should therefore be attributed, to a great extent, to the configuration of the submarine land; while currents give aid in preventing the closing of channels, and keeping open grounds for anchorage. This subject will be further illustrated in the following pages.

The permanency of coral harbors follows directly from the facts above presented. They are secure against any immediate obstruction from reefs. Any growing patches within them may still grow, and the margins of the enclosing reefs may gradually extend and contract their limits; yet only at an extremely slow rate. Notwithstanding such changes, the channels will remain open, and large anchorage grounds clear, as long as the currents continue in action. Coral harbors are therefore nearly as secure from any new obstructions as those of our continents. The growing of a reef in an adjoining part of the coast may in some instances diminish or alter the currents, and thus prepare the way for more important changes in the harbors; but such effects need seldom be feared, and results from them would be appreciable only after long periods, since the growth of reefs is very slow in the most favorable circumstances.

When channels have a bottom of growing coral, they form an exception to the above remark; for as the coral is acted upon by no cause sufficient to prevent its growth, the reef will continue to rise slowly towards the surface.

Again, when the channels are more than twenty fathoms in depth, they have an additional security beyond that from currents, in the fact that corals will not grow at such a depth. The only possible way in which such channels could close, without first filling up by means of shore material, would be by the extension of the reef from either side, till they bridge over the bottom below. But such an event is not likely to happen in any but very narrow channels.

In recapitulation, the existence of passages through reefs, and the character of coral harbors may be attributed to the following causes:

1. The configuration and character of the submarine land;—corals not growing where the depth exceeds certain limits, or where there is no firm basement for the plantation.

2. The direction and force of marine currents with their transported detritus;—these currents deriving their course, as in other regions, from the features of the land, the form of the sea-bottom and the reefs, and being sometimes increased in force by the contributions of island streams, which add to the detritus and to the weight of accumulating waters.

3. Harbors which receive freshwater streams or submarine springs of freshwater, are more apt to be clear from sunken patches; and the same causes keep open shallow passages to the shores, where there are shore reefs.

It should be remembered, that while the effects from freshwater streams are so trifling around islands, they may be of very wide influence on the shores of continents, where the streams are large and deep, and transport much detritus. This point is illustrated beyond.

b. Atoll Reefs.—The remarks in the preceding pages respecting reefs around other lands, apply equally to atoll reefs. There are usually currents flowing to leeward through the lagoon, and out, over or through the leeward reef, and this action, as with the coral harbor, tends to keep open a leeward channel for the passage of the water. This is the common explanation of the origin of the channels opening into lagoons. These currents are strongest when the windward reef is low, so as to permit the waves in some parts to break over it; and the coral debris they bear along will then be greatest. When a large part of the leeward reef is under water, or barely at the water's edge, the waters may escape over the whole, and on this account we sometimes find large reefs without any proper channels. As the land to windward becomes raised throughout above the sea, and forms a continuous line which the waves cannot pass, the current is less perfectly sustained, being dependent entirely upon the influx and efflux of the tides; and the leeward channels, in such a case, may gradually become closed.

The action of currents on atolls is, therefore, in every way identical with what has been explained. The absence of coves of land to give force to the waters of currents, and to direct their course, and the absence also of freshwater streams, are the only modifying causes not present. It is readily understood, therefore, why lagoon entrances are more likely to became filled up by growing coral, than the passages through barrier reefs.

3. *Rate of Growth of Reefs.*

The formation of a reef has been shown to be a very different process from the growth of a zoophyte. Its rate of progress is a question to be settled by a consideration of many distinct causes, and the rapid voyage of an Expedition affords no opportunity for definite conclusions.

a. The rapidity of the growth of zoophytes is an element in this question of great importance, and one that should be determined by direct observation with respect to each of the species which contribute largely to reefs, both in the warmer and colder parts of coral-reef seas.

b. The character of the coral plantation under consideration should be carefully studied: for it is of no little consequence to know whether the clusters of zoophytes are scattered tufts over a barren plain, or whether in crowded profusion. Compare the debris of vegetation on the semideserts of California with that of regions buried in foliage; equally various may be the rate of growth of coral rock in different places. Some allowance should also be made for the shells and other reef relics. The amount of reef rock formed in a given time cannot exceed, in cubic feet, the aggregate of corals and shells added by growth—that is, if there are no additions from other distant or neighboring plantations.

c. It is also necessary to examine into whatever has any bearing upon the marine or tidal currents of the region—their strength, velocity, direction, where they eddy, and where not, whether they flow over reefs that may afford debris or not. All the debris of one plantation may sometimes be swept away by currents to contribute to other patches, so that one will enlarge at the expense of others. Or, currents may carry the detritus into the channels or deeper waters around a coral patch, and leave little to aid the plantation itself in its increase and consolidation.

d. The course and extent of fresh waters from the land, and their detritus, should be ascertained.

e. The strength and height of the tides, and general force of the ocean waves, will have some influence.

Owing to the action of these causes, barrier reefs enlarge and extend more rapidly than inner reefs. The former have the full action of the sea, and are farther removed from the deleterious influences which may affect the latter.

As stated above, no results were arrived at from observations made in the course of the voyage through the Pacific. The general impression that their progress is slow, was fully sustained. The facts, with regard to the growth of zoophytes, give some data, though by no means satisfactory.

If we allow that Madrepores may grow three inches a year, it is far from admitting that a reef may increase as rapidly. In the best coral plantations, not over one-third of the surface is covered with growing zoophytes. It would therefore follow, supposing all the species to grow at this rate, and all the material to be retained on the plantation, that in twelve months the reef might possibly increase one inch in height; including shells and other animal remains, it might, perhaps, be one and one-quarter inches. This estimate is based on too many assumptions to be received with any confidence, except it be the confidence that the result is overrated.

With reference to this subject, by the order of Captain Wilkes a slab of rock was planted on Point Venus, Tahiti, and by soundings, the depth of Dolphin shoal, below the level of this slab, was carefully ascertained. By adopting this precaution, any error from change of level in the island, was guarded against: the slab remains as a stationary mark for future voyagers to test the rate of increase of the shoal. Before, however, the results can be of any general value towards determining the average rate of growing reefs, it is still necessary that the growing condition of the reef should be ascertained, the species of corals upon it be identified, and the influence of the currents investigated which sweep in that direction out of Matavai bay.

The depth to which Chamas or Tridacnas lie imbedded in coral rock, has been supposed to afford some data for estimating the growth of reefs. But Mr. Darwin rightly argues that these molluscs have the power of sinking themselves in the rock, as they grow, by removing the lime about them. They occur in the dead rock,—generally where there are no growing corals, except rarely some small tufts. If they indicate anything, it must be the growth of the reef rock, and not of the corals themselves. But the shore-platform where they are found is not increasing in height. They resemble, in fact, other saxicavous molluscs, several species of which are found in the same seas, some buried in the solid masses of dead coral lying on the reef. The bed they excavate for themselves is usually so complete that only an inch or two in breadth of their ponderous shells are exposed to view. Without some means like this of securing their habitations, these molluscs would be destroyed by the waves; a tuft of byssus, however strong, which answers for some small bivalves, would be an imperfect security against the force of the sea for shells weighing one to five hundred pounds.

4. *Origin of the Channels within Barriers, and of the Atoll Form of Coral Islands.*

In the review of causes modifying the forms of reefs, no reason was assigned for the most striking, we may say the most surprising, of all their features,—that they so frequently take a belt-like form, and enclose a wide lagoon; or in other cases, range along, at a distance of some miles, it may be, from the land they protect, with a deep sea separating them from the shores.

This peculiar character of the coral island was naturally the wonder of early voyagers, and the source of many speculations. The instinct of the polyp was made by some the subject of special admiration; for the "helpless animalcules" were supposed to have selected the very form best calculated to withstand the violence of the waves, and apparently with direct reference to the mighty forces which were to attack the rising battlements. They had thrown up a breastwork, as a shelter to an extensive working ground under its lee, "where their infant colonies might be safely sent forth."*

It has been a more popular theory that the coral structures were built upon the summits of volcanoes;—that the crater of the volcano corresponded to the lagoon, and the rim to the belt of land; that the entrance to the lagoon was over a break in the crater, a common result of an eruption. This view was apparently supported by the volcanic character of the high islands in the same seas.—But since a more satisfactory explanation has been offered by Mr. Darwin, numerous objections to this hypothesis have become apparent.

a. The volcanic cones must either have been subaerial and were afterwards sunk beneath the waters, or else they were submarine from the first. In the former case the crater would have been destroyed, with rare exceptions, during the subsidence; and in the latter there is reason to believe that a distinct crater would seldom, if ever, be formed.

b. The hypothesis, moreover, requires that the ocean's bed should have been thickly planted with craters—seventy in a single archipelago,—and they should have been of nearly the same elevation; for if more than twenty fathoms below the surface, corals could not grow upon them. But no records warrant the supposition that such a volcanic area ever existed. The volcanoes of the Andes differ from one to ten thousand feet in altitude, and scarcely two cones throughout the world are as nearly of the

* Flinders.

same height as here supposed. Mount Loa and Mount Kea, of Hawaii, present a remarkable instance of approximation, as they differ but two hundred feet: but the two sides of the crater of Mount Loa differ three hundred and fourteen feet in height. Mount Kea, though of volcanic character, has no large crater at top. Hualalai, the third mountain of Hawaii, is 4000 feet lower than Mount Loa. The volcanic summit of East Maui is 10,000 feet high, and is a fine example of a large crater; but the wall of the crater on one side is 700 feet lower than the highest point of the mountain; and the bottom of the crater is 2000 feet below the rim of the crater. Similar facts are presented by all volcanic regions.

c. It further requires that there should be craters at least fifty miles in diameter, and that twenty and thirty miles should be a common size. Facts give no support to such an assumption.

d. It supposes that the high islands of the Pacific, in the vicinity of the coral islands, abound in craters; while on the contrary there are none, as far as is known, in the Marquesas, Gambier, or Society Groups, the three which lie nearest to the Paumotus. Even this supposition fails, therefore, of giving plausibility to the crater hypothesis.

Thus at variance with facts, the theory has lost favor, and is no longer sustained even by those who were once its strongest advocates. The question still recurs with regard to the basement of coral islands, and the origin of their lagoon character. Shall we suppose, with some writers, that these islands were planted upon submarine banks, within one hundred and fifty feet of the surface of the sea? As has been said, there is no authority for the supposition. We nowhere find regions upon our continents with elevations so uniform in height; and submerged banks of this kind are of extremely rare occurrence. If such patches of submerged land existed, the lagoon structure would still be as inexplicable as ever; for the growing reefs of the Pacific show that corals may flourish alike over all parts of the bank, where not too deep. The zoophyte can by no means be said to prefer the declivity to the central plateau of the submarine bank: on the contrary, the part nearest the surface appears to abound in the largest species of corals.*

A study and comparison of the reefs of different kinds,—fringing, barrier, and atoll,—throughout the oceans, is the only philosophical mode of arriving at any conclusion on this subject. This course Mr. Darwin has happily and successfully pursued, and has arrived, as we have reason to believe, at the true theory of Coral Islands. It is satisfactory, because it is a simple generali-

* Lieutenant Nelson, R. N., suggested this hypothesis before the publication of Mr. Darwin's views. See Geol. Trans., vol. v, 12; and Darwin, op. cit., p. 94.

zation of facts. The explorations of the Expedition afford striking illustrations of his views, and elucidate some points which were still deemed obscure, establishing the theory on a firm basis of evidence, and exhibiting its complete correspondence with observation.

A. *Channels within barriers.*—We may turn again to the chart of the Feejee Group, and glance successively at the islands Goro, Angau, Nairai, Lakemba, Argo Reef, Exploring Isles, and Nanuku.* In Goro, the reef closely encircles the land upon whose submarine shores it was built up. In the island next mentioned, the reef has the same character, but is more distant from the shores, forming what has been termed a barrier reef; the name implying a difference in position, but none in mode of formation. In the last of the islands enumerated, the barrier reef includes a large sea, and the island it encloses is but a rocky peak within this sea.

Can we account for this diversity in the position of barrier reefs, and in their extent as compared with the enclosed land? There is evidently one way in which these features might have been produced. If, for example, such an island as Angau were very gradually to subside, from some subterranean cause, two results would take place:—the land would slowly disappear, while the coral reef, which is ever in constant increase, as has been explained, might retain itself at the surface, if the rapidity of subsidence was not beyond a certain rate. This subsidence might go on till the last mountain peak remained alone above the waters. Should we not then have a Nanuku? Suppose the subsidence not to have proceeded quite as far as this, it might leave only a single ridge and a few isolated summits peering above the waves. Would not its condition in this case be that of the Exploring Isles? On such a supposition, reefs of large size encircling a mere point of rock might be explained in every feature. The subsidence of Goro, on the same principle, would produce an Angau, or, carried further, a Nanuku.

It may here be remarked, that the fact that changes of level in the earth's surface have taken place over vast areas, is fully proved, and accounts of some of them which are now in progress, as that of Sweden, are to be found in any geological treatise.

But it admits of direct demonstration that such a subsidence has actually taken place. It has been stated that the depth of the reef at different distances from the shore it encircles may generally be estimated from the slope of the shore. On this principle it has been shown† that the thickness of the distant barrier reef cannot be less in some instances than a thousand feet; and

* This chart will be found in copies of the Narrative of the U. S. Exploring Expedition, by Capt. Wilkes, U. S. N.

† See page 19.

in many cases it is probably much greater. Now as reef corals do not grow below twenty fathoms, there is no way in which this thousand feet of reef could have been formed except by a gradual subsiding of the land upon which it stands. The large number of instances of distant barriers in the Pacific remove any doubt with regard to these conclusions. The map of the Feejees abounds in them through its eastern part, and we may infer with reason that this has been a large area of subsidence, like that which is now going on in Greenland.

Evidence of subsidence still more conclusive, if possible, is obtained by actual observation at Metia and some of the elevated coral islands. This island is 250 feet in height, full twice the coral-growing depth. At another island in the Hervey Group, Mangaia, the coral rock is raised 300 feet out of water.

The fact of subsidence having actually taken place during the formation of many reefs, is therefore put beyond doubt. It must form a part of any true theory of reefs, whether it be the crater hypothesis or the view here advocated. The latter has this advantage, that it explains all the facts, and requires no other element but this single one of subsidence. It rests on a simple fact and demands no hypothesis whatever.

The manner in which subsidence would operate is shown in the following sketches, representing ideal transverse sections of an island and its reefs. In figure 1, if I be the water line, the island, like Goro, has a simple fringing reef, *f*, *f*:—it is a narrow platform of rock at the surface, dropping off at its edge to shallow depths, and then some distance out, declining more abruptly. Let the same island become submerged till II is the water line:—the reef extends itself upward, as submergence goes on, and may have the character at the surface represented by $b' f' b' f'$. There is here a fringing reef and also a barrier reef, with a narrow channel between, such as we have described as existing on the shores of Tahiti;* b' is a section of the barrier, c' of the channel, and f' of the fringing reef. Suppose a farther submergence, till III is the water line: then the channel ($c'' c''$) within the barrier is quite broad, as in the island of Nairai or Angau; on one side (f'') the fringing reef remains, but on the other it has disappeared, owing, perhaps, to some change of circumstance as regards currents, which retarded its growth, and prevented its keeping pace with the subsidence. With the water at IV, there are two islets of rock in a wide lagoon, along with other islets ($i''' i'''$) of reef over two peaks which have disappeared. The coral reef-rock by gradual growth has attained a great thickness, and envelops nearly the whole of the former land. Nanuku, the Argo Reef, and Exploring Isles are here ex-

* See Page 14.

MAPS AND IDEAL SECTIONS OF CORAL REEFS AND ISLANDS.

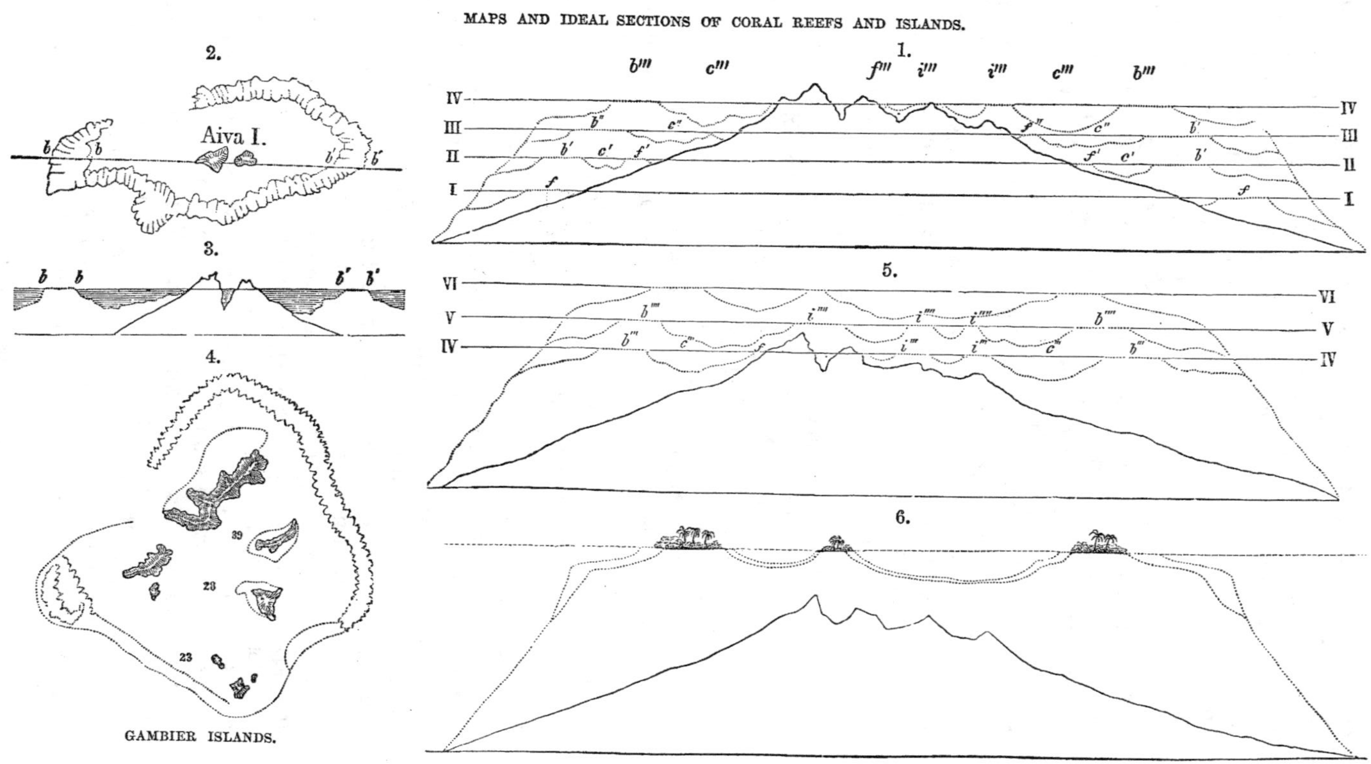

GAMBIER ISLANDS.

emplified, for the view is a good transverse section of either of them. $b''' \; b'''$ are sections of the distant enclosing barrier, and $c''' \; c'''$, and other intermediate spots, the water within.

The supposed similarity between these ideal sections and existing islands is fully sustained by actual comparison. Fig. 2 is a sketch of the island of Aiva in the Feejee Group. There are two peaks in the lagoon precisely as above; and although we have no soundings of the waters in and about it, nor sketches of peaks, facts observed elsewhere authorize in every essential point the transverse section given in figure 3, resembling closely, as is apparent, that in figure 1. The section is made through the line $b \; b$, $b' \; b'$, of figure 2. It is unnecessary to add other illustrations. They may be made out from any of the eastern groups of the Feejees, the Gambier Group of the Paumotus, or Hogoleu in the Carolines. Wallis's Island is another example of islets of rock in a large lagoon inclosed by a distant barrier.

It has been asked why the interior channels do not become filled by coral reef, as the island sinks, and thus a plane of coral result, instead of a narrow belt; and this has been urged against the theory of Mr. Darwin. But it is a sufficient reply to such an argument, to state the fact that the subsidence admits of no doubt, and that the islands referred to as exemplifications of it, present this very peculiarity. It should be received, therefore, as a consequence of it, instead of an objection to the view, for it is the most common feature with all islands that have broad reef-grounds, or in other words, that show evidence of subsidence during the growth of the reefs. Broad channels, and even open seas within, as in Nanuku and the Exploring Isles, are therefore to be received as results of the subsidence, for which explanations should be sought.

These explanations are at hand, and accord so exactly with facts ascertained, that the existence of inner passages becomes a necessary feature of such islands. It has been shown that the ocean acts an important part in reef-making;—that the outer reefs exposed to its action and to its pure waters, grow more rapidly than those within which are under the influence of marine and freshwater currents and transported detritus. It is obvious, therefore, that the former may retain themselves at the surface, when through a too rapid subsidence the inner patches would disappear. Moreover, after the barrier is once begun it has growing corals on both its inner and outer margin, while a fringing reef grows only on one margin. Again, the detritus of the outer reefs is, to a great extent, thrown back upon itself by the sea without and the currents within, while the inner reefs contribute a large proportion of their material to the wide channels between them. These channels, it is true, are filled in part from the outer reefs, but proportionally less from them than from the inner. The extent of reef-grounds within a barrier, raised by accumulations at the same time with the reefs, is often fifty times greater than the area of the barrier itself. Owing to these causes the rate of growth of the barrier may be at least twice more rapid than that of the inner reefs. If the barrier increases twenty feet in height in a century, the inner reef according to this supposition would increase but ten feet; and any rate of subsidence between the two mentioned, would sink the inner reefs more rapidly than they could grow, and cause them to disappear. A wide flat reef, continuous over so extensive reef-grounds, could be formed only with an extremely slow rate of subsidence; and even then they would be liable to be cut up by the production of inner currents, destroying growing corals over the interior parts of the coral reef; so that whatever the rate of subsidence, the inner portions would grow less rapidly. There is therefore not only no objection to the theory from the existence of wide channels and open seas; on the contrary, their non-existence is incompatible with the mode of action going on. They afford the strongest support to the theory.

From these considerations it is evident that a barrier reef indicates very nearly the former limits as to the land enclosed. The Exploring Islets, (Feejee chart,) instead of an area of *six* square miles, the whole extent of the existing land, once covered *three hundred* square miles; and the outline of the former land is indicated by the course of the enclosing reef. A still greater extent may be justly inferred. For the barrier, as subsidence goes on, gradually contracts its area, owing to the fact that the sea bears a great part of the material inward over the reefs: and, consequently, the declivity forming the outer limit of the submarine coral formation, has a steep angle of inclination.

In the same manner it follows that the island Nanuku, instead of *one* square mile, extended once over *two hundred* square miles, or had two hundred times the present area of high land. Bacon's Isles once formed a large triangular island of equal extent, though now but two points of rock remain above the water.

The two large islands in the western part of the group, Vanua Levu and Viti Levu, have distant barriers on the western side. Off the north point of the former, the reef begins to diverge from the coast, and stretches off from the shores till it is twenty and twenty-five miles distant; then, after a narrow interruption, without soundings, the Asaua islands commence in the same line, and sweep around to the reef which unites with the south side of Viti Levu; and tracing the reef along the south and east shores, we find it at last nearly connecting with a reef extending southward from Vanua Levu. Thus these two large islands are nearly encircled in a single belt; and it would be doing no violence to principles or probabilities, to suppose them once to have formed a single island, which subsidence has separated by inundating the low intermediate area. The singular reef of Whippey Harbor, p. 83, is fully explained by the hypothesis. We may thus not only trace out the general form of the land which once occupied this large area, (at least 10,000 square miles,) but may detect some of its prominent capes, as in Wakaia and Direction Island. The present area is not far from 4,500 square miles.

The whole Feejee Group, exclusive of coral islets, includes an area of about 5,500 square miles of dry land; while, at the period when the coral commenced to grow, there was, at least, as the facts show, 15,000 square miles of land, or nearly three times the present extent of surface.

B. *Lagoons of Atolls.*—We pass from these remarks on the channels and seas within barrier reefs, to the consideration of the seas or lagoons of coral atolls. The inference has probably been already made by the reader, that the same subsidence which has produced the distant barrier, if continued a step further, would produce the lagoon island. Nanuku is actually a lagoon island, with a single mountain peak still visible; and Nuku-Levu, north of it, is a lagoon island, with the last peak submerged. This mode of origin may evidently be true of all atolls; for with the exception of the points of high land in the inner waters, there is no one essential character, distinguishing many of the Eastern Feejee islands from the Carolines to the North. The Gambier group, near the Paumotus, appears to have afforded the philosophical mind of Mr. Darwin the first hint with regard to the origin of the atoll; the contrast, and, at the same time, the resemblance, was striking; the conclusion was natural and most happy.* As some interest is connected with the history of new principles, and the illustration afforded is highly satisfactory, we have given a sketch of the Gambier group, (fig. 4, p. 91.) The very features of the coast,—the deep indentations,—are sufficient evidence of subsidence to one who has studied the character of the Pacific islands:† for these indentations correspond to valleys or gorges formed by denudation, during a long period, while the island stood above the sea.

The manner in which a farther subsidence results in producing the atoll, may be illustrated by fig. 5, p. 91. Viewing V, as the water line, the land is entirely submerged; the barrier, b'''', b'''', is an angular reef, enclosing a broad area of waters, or a *lagoon*,

* Captain Beechey, in his voyage in the Pacific, implies this resemblance, when he says of the Gambier group, which he surveyed, "It consists of five large islands and several small ones, *all situated in a lagoon formed by a reef of coral*,"—p. 120, Amer. ed. Balbi, the geographer, as Mr. Darwin remarks, describes those barrier reefs which encircle islands of moderate size, by calling them atolls, with high lands rising from their central expanse.—Darwin, op. cit., p. 41.

† This subject is discussed in the chapter, on the author's Geological Report, on the valleys of the Pacific islands.

with a few island patches of reef over the peaks of the mountains.* At a still greater subsidence (to the line VI) the islets, excepting one, have disappeared, owing to their increasing less rapidly than the barrier. The lagoon is in exact correspondence, in all its characters, with those of atoll reefs. Should subsidence now cease, the reefs, no longer increasing in height, would go on to widen, and the accumulations produced by the sea would commence the formation of dry land, as exhibited in figure 6, (p. 91.) Verdure may soon after appear, and the coral island is finally completed. It is not impossible that the land should form in certain favorable spots, while the subsidence is in progress if it be not beyond a certain rate.

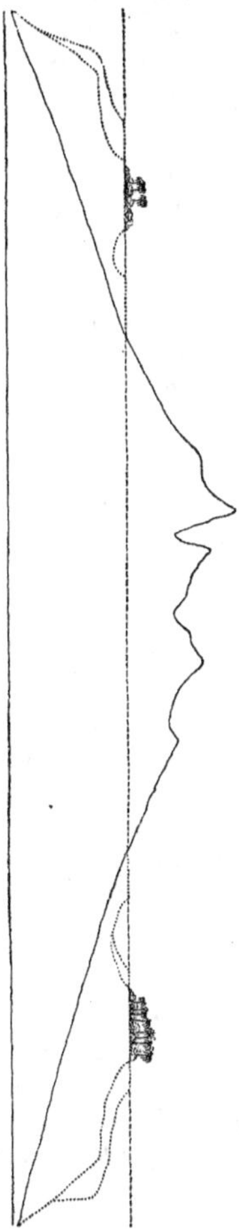

The annexed figure represents the effect of a cessation or diminution of subsidence on the barrier reef, about a high island. The barrier reef has become a finished island, and forms a green belt to the land. The figure shows a section of such a belt.

All the features of atolls harmonize completely with this view of their origin. In form they are as various and irregular as the outlines of barrier reefs. Compare Angau of the Feejees, with Tari-tari of the Tarawan Group; Nairai or Moala with Tarawa; Nanuku with Maiana or Apamama. The resemblance is close; and in the same manner we might find all the forms of lagoon reefs represented among barrier reefs. We observe all those configurations which would be derived from land of various shapes of outline, whether the narrow mountain ridge, (as at Taputeouea, one of the Tarawan Islands,) or wide areas of irregular slopes and mountain ranges. Among the groups of high islands, we observe that abrupt shores may occasion the absence of a reef on one side, as on Moala; and a like interruption is found among coral islands. Many of the passages through the reefs may be thus accounted for.

The fact that the submerged reef is often much prolonged from the capes or points of a coral island, accords well with

* As the lagoon islets cover the summits of the subsided mountains, they afford the most favorable spots for reaching the rocks below by boring. In fig. 6, p. 91, the depth required for this purpose on an islet in the lagoon would be hardly a fourth what would be necessary on the enclosing reef.

these views. These points or capes correspond to points in the original land, and often to the line of the prominent ridge; and it is well known that such ridge-lines often extend a long distance with slight inclination compared with the slopes or declivities bounding the ridge on either side.

Coral islands or reefs often lie in chains like the peaks of a single mountain range:—for example, the sickle-shape line of islets north of Nanuku. Taritari and Makin, (Tarawan group, see map at the end,) lie together as if belonging to parts of one island. Menchicoff atoll, in the Caroline Archipelago, consists of three long loops or lagoon islands, united by their extremities, and further subsidence might reduce it to three islands.*

The sizes of atolls offer no objection to these views, as they do not exceed those of many barrier reefs. Some of the larger Maldives, according to the crater theory, would require a crater seventy miles in diameter, with a rim made up of subordinate craters. No hypothesis of such extravagance is necessary. The facts all fall in with known principles, and are illustrated by known and established truths, without hypotheses of any kind.

It is of some interest to follow still further the subsidence of a coral island, the earlier steps in which are illustrated in the preceding figures. One obvious result of its continuation is a gradual contraction of the lagoon and diminution of the size of the atoll, owing to the fact already noted, that the detritus is mostly thrown inward by the sea. The lagoon will consequently become smaller and shallower, and the outline of the island in general more nearly circular. Finally, the reefs of the different sides may so far approximate by this process, that the lagoon is gradually obliterated, and the large atoll is thus reduced to a small level islet, with only traces of a former depression about the centre. Thus subsidence is connected with detritus accumulations in filling up the lagoon; and as filled lagoons are found only in the smallest islands, such as Swains and Jarvis, the two agencies have beyond doubt been generally united.

This subsidence, if more rapid than the increase of the coral reef, becomes fatal to the atoll, by gradually sinking it beneath the sea. Of this character evidently is the Chagos Bank.† The southern Maldives have deeper lagoons than the northern, fifty

---

* See Darwin on the probable disseverment of the Maldives, op. cit., p. 37, in which he points out indications of a breaking up of a large atoll into several smaller. A land with many summits or ranges of heights may at first have its single enclosing reef; but as it subsides, this reef contracting upon itself may encircle separately the several ranges of which the island consisted, and thus several atoll reefs may result in place of the large one; and further, each peak may finally become the basis of a separate lagoon island, under a certain rate of subsidence or variations in it, provided the outer reef is so broken as to admit the influence of waves and winds. The Maldives are a good example of this result. Some of the large atolls are properly atoll archipelagos.

† For a detailed account of this and other submerged reefs, see Darwin, p. 106.

or sixty fathoms being found in them. This fact indicates that subsidence was probably most extensive to the south, and perhaps also most rapid. The sinking of the Chagos Bank still further south, in nearly the same line, may therefore have some connection with the subsidence of the Maldives.

In view of the facts which have been presented, it appears that each coral atoll once formed a fringing reef around a high island. The fringing reef, as the island subsided, became a barrier reef, which continued its growth while the land was slowly disappearing. The area of waters within finally contained the last sinking peak: another period, and this had gone—the island had sunk, leaving only the barrier at the surface and an islet or two of coral in the enclosed lagoon. Thus the coral wreath thrown around the lofty island to beautify and protect, becomes afterwards its monument, and the only record of its past existence. The Paumotu Archipelago is a vast island cemetery, where each atoll marks the site of a buried island. The whole Pacific is scattered over with these simple memorials, and they are the brightest spots in that desert of waters.

5. *Geographical Distribution of Coral Reefs and Islands.*

THE distribution of coral reefs over the globe depends on the following circumstances, arising from the habitudes of polyps already explained:

1. The temperature of the ocean.
2. The character of coasts as regards (*a*) the depth of water, —(*b*) the nature of the shores,—(*c*) the presence of streams.
3. Liability to exposure to destructive agents, such as volcanic heat.

It has been stated that reef-growing corals* will flourish in the hottest seas of the equator, and over the ocean wherever the winter temperature is not below 66° F. The isocheimal line of this temperature therefore forms the boundary line of the coral-reef seas.

This line traverses the oceans between the parallels 26° and 30°, or in general near 28°. But in the vicinity of the continents it undergoes remarkable flexures, from the influence of oceanic currents, the polar currents bending it towards the equator, while the tropical cause a divergence. From a comparison of the thermometrical observations of various voyagers with those of the Expedition, I have been enabled to draw this coral boundary with a considerable degree of accuracy; and it is laid

* There are corals in colder seas; we here refer to those species that form reefs.

down upon the chart of the world accompanying my Report. In the Pacific it is observed to exclude the Galapagos,* and reach the South American coast *north* of the equator, instead of at the parallel of 28° south, the position in mid-ocean. On the coast of Asia it curves *from* the equator beyond latitude 30°. In the Atlantic it forms an abrupt bend far to the north, in the line of the Gulf Stream, and includes the Bermudas in latitude 32° N.; while on the African coast the northern line curves downward to the latitude of the Cape Verds, and the southern upward nearly to the equator. The following table will give more definitely the position of the coral boundary line where it meets the coasts of the continents.

	Pacific Ocean.	Atlantic Ocean.
East side of ocean—Northern,	Latitude 21° N.	Latitude 10° N.
Southern.	4° N.	5° S.
West side of ocean—Northern.	34° N.	34° N.
Southern.	30° S., New Holland. 29° S., Africa.	22° S.

It follows from the above, that while the coral-reef seas are about fifty-six degrees wide in mid-ocean, they are *in the Pacific* seventeen degrees wide on the west coast of America, and sixty-four degrees on the Asiatic side. *In the Atlantic*, they are about fifteen degrees wide on the African coast, and fifty-six degrees on the coast of America. If we reckon to the extremity of the bend in the Gulf Stream, the whole width off the east coast of America, north of the equator, will be over forty degrees. It is obvious that these facts enable us to explain many seeming anomalies in the distribution of coral reefs.

Within the limits included by the coral-reef boundary line, those other causes operate which influence the distribution of reefs. The effect of a deep abrupt coast has been pointed out. The unfavorable character of sandy or muddy shores, and the action of detritus, marine currents, and fresh waters have also been stated.

No less striking are the effects of *volcanic action* in preventing the formation of reefs; and instances of this influence are numerous throughout the Pacific. The existence of narrow reefs, or their entire absence, may often be thus accounted for. For example, in the Sandwich Group, the island Hawaii, still active with volcanic fires, has but few traces of corals about it, while the westernmost islands, which have been longest free from such action, have reefs of considerable extent. The island of Maui

* Captain Fitzroy, R.N., found the surface temperature of the sea at the Galapagos, from Sept. 16 to Oct. 18, 1835, 62° to 70° F. Oct. 23, in lat. 0° 30′ S., and long. 99° 4′ W., the temperature of the sea was 66° F. Oct. 24, lat. 0° 23′ N., long. 96° 53′ W., temp. 70½°, 71½° F. While under the equator, about the middle of the Pacific, the range of surface temperature of the sea through the year is 81° to 88° F.

exemplifies well the general fact. The island consists of two peninsulas: one, the eastern, recent volcanic, with a large crater at summit, and the other, the western, presenting every evidence in its gorges and peaks and absence of volcanic cones, of having become extinct ages since. In conformity with the view expressed, the coral reefs are confined almost exclusively to the latter peninsula. Other examples are afforded by the Samoan Islands. Savaii abounds in extinct craters and lava streams, and much resembles Hawaii in character: it bears proof in every part of being the last seat of the volcanic fires of Samoa. Its reefs are consequently few and small: there is but a narrow line on part of the northern shores, although on the other islands they are very extensive. The absence of corals results obviously from the destruction of zoophytes by heat, consequent on volcanic action. Submarine eruptions, which are frequent as long as a volcano near the sea is in action, heat the waters, and destroy whatever of life they may contain: after the eruption of Kilauea, in 1840, there were numerous dead fish thrown on the beach; and many such instances in different regions are on record. Other facts, illustrating the effects of volcanic heat in preventing the growth of reefs, will be brought forward in the following pages.

The agencies affecting the growth of coral reefs being before the mind, we may proceed to notice the actual distribution of reefs through the coral seas. The review given is a rapid one, as our present object is simply to explain the absence or presence of reefs within the coral reef limits, by reference to the above facts.*

Pacific Ocean.—The west coast of South America is known to be without coral reefs even immediately beneath the equator; and the seas of the Galapagos also grow no coral. The northward deflection of the coral boundary line, as shown, accounts for their absence. In the harbor of Callao (the seaport of Lima), the temperature is sometimes down to 59° or 60° F., and at the Galapagos, Captain Fitzroy found the waters in September to fall often to 62° F., and once to 58½ F. This month, it should be observed, cannot be the coldest of the year. In the bay of Panama, coral is reported to occur, but there are no reefs.†

---

* In the valuable work by Mr. Darwin, the geographical distribution of reefs is treated of at length in the Appendix, pp. 151-205. The facts here detailed have been obtained from independent sources, except where otherwise acknowledged. In accounting for the character and distribution of reefs, Mr. Darwin has erred in attributing too much weight to a supposed difference in the amount of subsidence in different regions, neglecting to allow the requisite limiting influence to volcanic agency, and to the other causes mentioned.

† Jour. Roy. Geog. Soc., i, 69, on the Isthmus of Panama, by J. A. Lloyd.

The coast to the north, as far as latitude 21° N., is within the warm limits, but without reefs. In Captain Colnett's voyage, allusion is made to a beach of coral sand on one of the Revillagigedo Islands, in latitude 18°; beside this statement, I have met with no allusion to corals on any of the islands off the Mexican coast. The paucity of corals in this region may perhaps be owing, in some degree, to the fact that the tropical currents of the ocean flow *westward* instead of eastward; and, consequently, they prove an obstable to the distribution of polyps to this coast from the islands of the Pacific. Moreover, the cold currents which pass the Galapagos form an impassable barrier between the Paumotus and Mexico.

Between the South American coast and the Paumotus are two rocky islands, Easter or Waihu, and Sala-y-Gomez, both of which are without reefs.*

The Paumotus commence in longitude 130° W., and embrace eighty coral islands, all of which, excepting about eight of small size, contain lagoons. Besides these, there are, near the southern limits of the archipelago, the Gambier Islands, and Pitcairn, of basaltic constitution. The former, in 23° S., have extensive reefs; about the latter, in 25° S., there are some growing corals, but no proper reefs.

The Marquesas, in latitude 10° S., have but little coral about them; and this is the more remarkable, as they are in close proximity to the Paumotus. But their shores are, in general, very abrupt, with deep waters close to the rocks. An island which, before subsidence has commenced, has some extent of shallow waters around, might have very bold shores, after it had half sunk beneath the waves. This would be the case with the island of Tahiti; for its mountain declivities are, in general, singularly precipitous, except at base. The Marquesas may, therefore, have once had barrier reefs, which were sunk from too rapid subsidence; and afterwards, on the cessation of the subsidence, others failed to form again, on account of the deep waters.

The Society Islands have extensive coral reefs, with distant barriers. The reefs of Tahiti extend, in some parts, a mile from the shores. Tethuroa, to the north of Tahiti, and Tubuai, near Bolabola, are lagoon islands. Maitea, east of Tahiti, is a sugarloaf truncated at summit, four miles in compass, and is said by Forster to have an encircling reef.†

South of the Society Islands, near 25° S., is Rapa, which is represented as a collection of rugged peaks without coral shores. The Rurutu and Hervey Islands, just northwest of Rapa, have coral reefs fringing the shores. There is no evidence of recent

* Captain Beechey mentions that at forty-one fathoms, near Sala-y-Gomez, he found a bottom of sand and coral.

† Darwin, op. cit., p. 153.

volcanic action among them. Some of them are elevated coral islands, as Mitiaro, Atiu, Mangaia and Mauki, and also, according to Stutchbury, Rurutu. Okatutaia is a low coral island but six or seven feet out of water.

Between the Paumotus and the longitude of Samoa, are numerous small islands, all of coral origin.

The Samoan Islands have extensive reefs. About Tutuila they are somewhat less extensive than around Upolu, owing to its abrupt shores; and about Savaii they are still smaller, as already explained. The influence of abrupt shores may also be seen in some parts of Upolu; for example, to the west of the harbor of Falifa, where, for several miles, there is no reef, except in some of the indentations of the coast. Manua is described as having only shore reefs.*

The Tonga Islands, south of Samoa, for the most part, abound in coral reefs, and Tongatabu and the Hapai Group are solely of coral. Eoa is a moderately high island, with a narrow reef. Tafoa, an active volcano, and Kao an extinct cone, are *without* reefs. Vavau, according to Williams,† is an elevated coral island. Pylstaarts, near Eoa, is a naked rock, with abrupt shores, and little or no coral. Sunday Island, farther south, (29° 12′ S.,) is beyond the coral-reef limits.

North of Samoa are several scattered islands of small size, all of coral.

The Feejee Group, as we have sufficiently described, abounds in reefs of great extent. There are no active volcanoes, and, where examined, no evidence of very recent volcanic action. The many islands afford a peculiarly favorable region for the growth of zoophytes, and the displays of reefs and living corals were the most remarkable seen by the writer in the Pacific.

North of the Feejees are numerous islands, leading up to the Carolines. They are all of coral, excepting Rotuma, Horne and Wallis's Islands, which are high, and have fringing or barrier reefs. The reefs of Wallis Island are very extensive.

The Tarawan Islands, and the Carolines including the Marshall Islands, eighty-seven in number, are all atolls, excepting the three Carolines, Ascension or Banabe, (Pouynipete of Lutke,) Ualan, and Hogoleu (or Roug).

The westernmost of the Sandwich Islands, Kauai and Oahu, have fringing reefs, while eastern Maui and the island of Hawaii have but few traces of corals. On Hawaii, the only spot of reef seen by us, was a submerged patch off the southern cape of Hilo Bay. We have already attributed the absence of corals to the volcanic character of the island. The small islands to the north-

---

* Narrative Expl. Exp., by C. Wilkes, U. S. N., ii, 65.

† Miss. Enterprises, p. 427, Amer. ed.

west of Kauai, are represented as coral reefs, excepting the rocks Necker and Bird Island; the line stretches on to 28° 30′ N.,* the northern limit of the coral seas.

The Ladrones, like the Sandwich Group, constitute a line or linear series of islands, one end of which has been long free from volcanic action, while the other has still its smoking cones. While the appearances of recent igneous action increase therefore as we go northward, the extent of the coral reefs increase as we go southward; no reefs occur about the northernmost islands, while they are quite extensive on the shores of Guam. This group consequently, like the Hawaiian and Samoa, illustrates the influence of volcanic action on the distribution of reefs.

A short distance southwest of the Ladrones, and nearly in the same line, lie extensive reefs. Mackenzie's is an atoll of large size. Yap, Hunter, Los Matelotas and the Pelews are high islands, with large reefs. In the last mentioned, the reef-grounds cover at least six times the area occupied by the high land. Still farther south, towards New Zealand, lie the large atolls Aiou, Asie, and Los Guedes.

South of the equator again:—The New Hebrides constitute a long group of high islands, remarkable for the absence of coral reefs of any extent, though situated between two of the most extensive coral regions in the world,—the Feejees and New Caledonia. But the volcanic nature of the group, and the still active fires of two vents in opposite extremities are a sufficient reason for this peculiarity. Tanna is one of the largest volcanoes of the Pacific; and nearly all the islands of the New Hebrides, as far as known, indicate comparatively recent igneous action, in which respect they differ decidedly from the Feejees.

The Vanikoro Group, north of the New Hebrides, according to Quoy, has large barrier reefs about the southernmost island, Vanikoro; but at the northern extremity of the range there is an active volcano Tinakoro, and no coral. Tikopia, to the southeast of Vanikoro, is high and volcanic, according to Quoy, though not now with active fires; and it appears from the descriptions given to have no reefs. Mendana, northeast of Tinakoro, according to Kruesenstern, as stated by Darwin, is low with large reefs; Duff's Islands have bold summits with wide reefs.

New Caledonia and the northeast coast of New Holland, with the intermediate seas, constitute one of the grandest reef regions in the world. On the New Caledonia shores the reefs are of great width, and not only occur along the whole length of the western coast, a distance of 200 miles, but extend to the south beyond the main land 50 miles, and north 150 miles, making in

* For an account of some of these islands, see Lisiansky's Voyage, 1803–6, in the Neva, 4to., London, 1814, pp. 254, 257; also Hawaiian Spectator, vol. i.

all a line of reef full 400 miles in length. Towards the north extremity, however, it is interrupted or broken into detached reefs. This surprising extent is partly explained by the fact that New Caledonia is not a land of volcanoes; but on the contrary, consists of the older Plutonic or metamorphic rocks, with probably some sedimentary rocks. The streams of so large a land might be expected to exclude reefs from certain parts: and in accordance with this fact, we find the reefs of the windward or rainy side comparatively small, and scarcely indicated on our charts; while on the dry or western side, they often extend 30 miles from the shores. The theory of subsidence accounts fully for the great prolongation of the New Caledonia reefs; they indicate, moreover, the existence of a former land near three times the area of the present island.

Between New Caledonia and the New Hebrides are several high islands, one of which, *Lafu*, has been recently described by Rev. W. B. Clarke as an elevated coral island, with fringing reefs; and it appears also from the remarks of this writer, that the other islets of what is called the Loyalty Group, are of the same kind. Lafu, the largest of the number, is about ninety miles in circumference.*

South of New Caledonia lies Norfolk Island, in latitude 29° S., about which there is said to be some coral, which is occasionally thrown on the beach, but no reefs.

Between Australia and New Caledonia the islands are all of coral. The New Holland reef extends from Torres Straits to the east cape in latitude 24° S., a distance of 1000 nautical miles, though much interrupted along its course. It has been shown how this broken character might result during a subsidence, owing to a change in the abruptness of the land successively becoming the coast line, and also to the variations in the currents, retarding the growth in some places and aiding it in others. These causes might make a broken reef of one that was originally continuous: yet we have no reason to believe that the reef was ever continuous. It will be found, as we proceed, that long reefs on the shores of continents are not common. In this case the zoophytes are not exposed to the destructive agents usual on such shores, as the land is in a dry climate, the shores are mostly rocky, and there are no streams of any extent emptying into the ocean. The east cape is the southern limit, because here the tropical current, owing to the direction of the coast above, trends off to the eastward of south, away from the land, while a polar current follows up the shores from the south as far as this cape. South of this cape there are only a few scattered species of coral zoophytes.

The Louisiade Group is described as a region of extensive reefs.

---

* Quarterly Journal of the Geological Society, No. 9, p. 61.

The Salomon Islands, as far as ascertained, are but sparingly fringed, except the two westernmost, which are said to have large reefs. The peculiar character of these lands is too imperfectly known to allow of our deducing the cause of so restricted reefs. Off to the north of the Salomon Islands, there are several atolls of considerable size. New Ireland, according to D'Urville, has distant reefs on part of its shores.

The Admiralty Islands, farther west, are enclosed by barrier reefs, and beyond this group there are a few lagoon islands.

The north side of New Guinea is mostly without coral. There are several islands off this coast, which are conical volcanic summits, and one of them, near New Britain, and another (Vulcano), near longitude 145° E., are in action.

From the facts thus far detailed, the connection between the prevalence or extent of reefs, and the various causes assigned as limiting or promoting their growth, is obvious. The amount of subsidence determines in some cases the distance of barrier reefs from shores; but it by no means accounts for the difference in their extent in different parts of a single group of islands. Indeed, if this cause be considered alone, every grade of extent, from no subsidence to the largest amount, might in many instances be proved as having occurred on a single island. Of far greater importance, as has appeared, is the volcanic character of the land. At whatever time the existing reefs in the Pacific commenced their growth, they began about those of the igneous islands whose fires had become nearly or quite extinct; and as others in succession were extinguished, these became in their turn the sites of corals, and reefs began to form. Those lands whose volcanoes still burn, are yet without corals, or there are only limited patches on some favored spots. Zoophytes and volcanoes are the land-making agents of the Pacific. The latter prepare the way by pouring forth the liquid rock, and building up the lofty summit. Quiet succeeds, and then commences the work of the zoophyte beneath the sea, while verdure covers the exposed heights.

We may add a few more illustrations from other parts of the coral-reef seas.

Along the north and northwest coast of New Holland, there appears to be little or no coral in the Gulf of Carpentaria, while some extensive patches occur on the shores west of this Gulf, as far as the northwest cape in latitude 23° S.

In the East Indies, there are large, scattered reef-islands, south of Borneo and Celebes, and the west end of New Guinea. The islands of Timor-laut, and Timor, with many of those intermediate, have large reefs. The Arru Group consists wholly of coral. This sea, from Arru to the islands south of Borneo, is more thriving in corals than any other in the East Indies.

Another East Indian coral reef region, of some extent, is the Sooloo Sea, between Mindanao and the north of Borneo. Yet the reefs are mostly submerged. We saw no wide platforms bordering the high lands, like those of the Pacific. There are, however, some small coral islets in the Balabac Passage.

In other parts of the East Indies, coral reefs are quite inconsiderable. Occasional traces, sometimes amounting to a fringing reef, occur along Luzon and the other Philippines.

We coasted by the west shore of Luzon to Manila, and thence by Luban, Mindoro, Panay, to Caldera, near Samboangan in Mindanao; and through this distance, no reefs were distinguished, as would have been the case had there been any of much extent. At the last mentioned place we found coral pebbles on the beach, and by dredging obtained living specimens in six to eight fathoms of water. The only large reefs were those between Mindoro and the Calaminianes. There are fringing reefs at Singapore. The islands of Borneo, Celebes, Java, and Sumatra, according to all the authorities seen by the writer, have but few coral patches about their shores, although affording long lines of coast for their growth. In the China Seas, there are numerous shoals, banks and island reefs of coral. Moreover, shore-reefs occur about Loochoo, and the islands between it and Formosa. But the whole eastern coast of China appears to be without coral. Quelpaert's island, south of Corea, in 34° N., is described as having coral about it; and this has been confirmed by late information.

Why should the reefs of the East India Archipelago be so limited in extent, and large parts be almost destitute, notwithstanding their situation in the warmest seas of the ocean, and in the most favorable region for tropical productions? We are not prepared for a full answer to this inquiry, which demands a thorough knowledge of the shores, as well as of the currents, and of the former and present condition of volcanic fires. From personal observation, we may reply satisfactorily, as far as regards part of the southern half of the east coast of Sumatra. This coast is low, and sandy or muddy, and thus affords the most unfavorable place for zoophytes. A strong current sweeps through the straits of Banka, which keeps the water muddy, and the shores in constant change. The same cause may operate on the coasts of other islands, but we are ignorant to what extent.

The East Indies have been remarkable for their volcanoes, exceeding, for the area, every other part of the world: and this fact must have influence on the formation of coral reefs, though we have not the data for fixing the extent of the influence. Of the thousand vents which have been in action, several still make themselves felt over wide areas. The Sooloo islands are about one hundred in number, and nearly all are pointed with volcanic cones; and while some have the broken declivities that are marks of age, others have regular slopes, as if but just now extinguished: a dozen of these cones may sometimes be seen on a single island. These volcanic peaks often rise out of the sea, as if their formation had begun with a submarine eruption. In a region so extensively and so recently igneous, the coral polyp would have found little chance to develop itself, until volcanic action had become comparatively quiet, and deluges of hot water ceased. There appears, therefore, to be some reason for the fact that the reefs are small, and have seldom reached the surface.

The Sooloo Sea is but one of the volcanic clusters in these seas. Java, several of the Philippines, and other islands south of these last, with the northern shore of New Guinea, make up a wide region of fires, and it cannot be doubted that the frequent eruptions prevented the growth of coral, for a long period, over large areas. For other causes we must look to the nature of the coasts, fresh-water streams and marine currents; we leave it for other investigators to apply the explanation to particular coasts.

The coast of China probably owes its freedom from corals to its alluvial character and its fresh-water streams.

One interesting fact should be noted:—the most extensive reefs in the East Indies are to be found in the open seas, between the large islands; these islands, at the same time, often being without proper reefs, or with mere traces of coral. This is the case between Borneo and the range of large islands south: the China Sea is another instance of it; north of New Guinea, a few degrees, is another. How far this is due to their being distant from the scenes of igneous action, and from the detritus and fresh-water of island streams, remains to be determined. A sinking island becomes a more and more favorable spot for the growth of coral, as it descends; for as its extent diminishes, its streams of fresh-water and detritus also decrease. It might therefore be expected, on this account alone, that such isolated spots of land, away from all impure waters, in the open ocean, should become the bases of large reefs. The existence of these reef-islands is, therefore, no necessary proof of greater subsidence than the coast adjoining has undergone, though the fact of a greater subsidence is by no means impossible.

In the Indian Ocean, the Asiatic coast is mostly free from growing coral.* The great rivers of the Continent are probably the most efficient cause of their absence, both directly, through their fresh waters, and through the detritus they transport and distribute along the shores. It will be observed that this agent, so ineffectual on small islands, is one of vast influence upon larger lands. Ceylon has some fringing reefs.

* Mr. Darwin alludes to small patches in the Persian Gulf.

The islands of the Indian Ocean are, to a great extent, purely of coral. Of this character are the Laccadives, Maldives, Keelings, Saya-de-Malha, Almirante, and Cosmoledo. The Chagos shoal is of the same character: and the shoal Cargados is probably similar. The Seychelles are small islands with extensive reefs. We remark here the same fact alluded to above, that reefs abound in the open ocean, though absent from the Continental coasts; and the same reason may apply to both cases.

Madagascar has a fringing reef upon its southwestern point, according to Mr. Darwin, and on some parts of the coast above; also on the north and eastern shores far down as latitude 18° S.* The Comoro Islands, between Madagascar and the continent, have large barrier reefs.

The eastern coast of Africa has narrow reefs extending north with some interruptions from Mozambique, in latitude 16° S., to a short distance from the equator. Corals also abound in the Red Sea, occurring in some parts on both shores, though most frequent on the eastern, from Tor, in the Gulf of Suez, to Konfodah. This long continental reef may at first be deemed a little remarkable, after what we have remarked upon such reefs elsewhere. Yet the surprise is at once set aside by the striking fact that this whole coast, from the isthmus of Suez south, has no rivers, excepting some inconsiderable streams. It affords, therefore, an interesting elucidation of the subject under consideration, and confirms the view taken to account for the absence of reefs from the China and South Asiatic coasts. It is a fact almost universal, that where there are large fresh water streams, there are earthy or sandy shores; and where there are no such streams, rocky shores, though not uniformly occurring, are common.

Passing from the Indian to the Atlantic Ocean, we find little or no coral on the west coast of Africa. The islands of Cape St. Anne and Sherboro, south of Sierra-Leone, are described as coral by Captain Owen, R.N.† But this has been since denied. The island of Ascension, in 7° 56′ S., and 14° 16′ W., must have been formerly bordered by growing coral, as Quoy and Gaymard mention that a bed of coral rock may be seen buried beneath streams of lava. Quoy also states that the corals which formed these reefs are no longer found alive, and adds that volcanic eruptions have probably destroyed them. The cold polar currents along the African coast, although generally leaving about fifteen degrees of latitude within the coral-reef seas, may at times close up and reduce it to still narrower limits. The same obstacle to the diffusion of species eastward, mentioned as occurring in the Pacific—that is, westerly currents—exists also in the Atlantic, and probably with the same effect.

---

* Darwin, op. cit., p. 187.

† Journal of the Royal Geographical Society, ii, 89.

On the American shores of the Atlantic there are few reefs, except in the West Indies. The waters of the Orinoco and Amazon, and the alluvial shores they occasion, exclude corals from that part of the coast. But about Pernambuco, as I am informed by Mr. Titian R. Peale, there are some patches of growing corals, and they are said to extend along to 20° or 21° S.

The Bermudas are of coral origin, and are the most northern point of growing reefs.

In the West Indies, the reefs of Key West, Cuba, the Bahamas, and many of the eastern islands are well known. On the east coast of Florida they continue up as far as Cape Florida, in latitude 25° 40′ N.: the west coast is free of them. There are also said to be patches at intervals along the coast of Venezuela and Guatemala; but the west shores of the Gulf of Mexico, as well as the northern, like West Florida, are mostly low, and everywhere without corals. They are within the influence of the Mississippi and other large rivers.

We have thus seen that the earth is belted by a coral zone, corresponding nearly to the tropics in extent, and that the oceans throughout it abound in zoophyte reefs, wherever congenial sites are afforded for their growth. We have found that the currents of extra-tropical seas, which flow westward, and are interrupted and trended *towards* the equator by the continents, contract the coral seas in width, narrowing them to a few degrees on the western coasts of the continents; while the tropical currents, flowing eastward, *diverge* from the equator and cause the belt to widen near the eastern shores. The polar currents flow also by the eastern coasts, preventing the warmer waters from increasing the width of the coral zone as much as it is contracted on the western coasts. Moreover, the trend and capes of the coast produce other modifications in the direction of the currents, the most of which are apparent in the actual distribution of coral reefs. On the shores of the continents we have observed that there are no extensive reefs, except along eastern Africa; and, while other lands abound in rivers, this African coast has only some comparatively small streams. Thus the influence of continental waters and detritus on the distribution of reefs, has been shown to be very marked. But about the Pacific islands, where streams are small, the same cause has had little effect, seldom doing more than modifying somewhat the shores and bottom of a harbor. We have ascertained that in different groups, as the Ladrones, the Sandwich Islands, Samoa, New Hebrides, there is an inverse relation between the extent of reefs and the evidences of recent volcanic action in the island; and that the largest reefs exist where there is no proof of former igneous action, or where it has long ceased. The adverse influence of volcanic agency to the planting and increase of coral reefs is thus satisfactorily exhibited. The existence of large reef-islands in open seas, where the neighboring lands are mostly destitute of coral reefs, has farther supported our conclusions, as such islands are in general removed from the deleterious influences just mentioned.

The modifications of form and interruptions of reefs arising from abrupt or sloping shores, and tidal or local currents, have also been exemplified. The origin of the distant barrier has been traced to a sinking of the land which it once simply fringed; and the lagoon island to a continuation of this subsidence till the original land had disappeared.

This account of coral reefs and islands may be closed by a statement or recapitulation of some deductions which have a special bearing upon geology.

CHAPTER IV.

GEOLOGICAL CONCLUSIONS FROM THE STRUCTURE AND COMPOSITION OF CORAL REEFS AND ISLANDS.

The geological bearing of the facts that have been detailed, has probably been already perceived by our readers. A brief recapitulation, however, may afford a convenient review of the subject. The following are the points of more special interest.

I. The *coral reef-rock* has been described as solid limestone of coral origin. In some parts it is a coral conglomerate, or breccia, made up of fragments firmly cemented. Over much larger areas it is a fine white limestone, as compact as any secondary marble, and as homogeneous in texture. It is often free from any traces of organic life, or proofs of an organic origin. Only now and then an imbedded shell or some other relic evinces that animals of any kind were living in the seas. This white limestone breaks with a conchoidal fracture, a splintery surface, and rings under the hammer. These facts are of great importance in deciding upon the origin of the older limestone strata. Other portions of the rock, of less extent, are made of standing corals with the intervals filled in by reef-debris, and the whole cemented solid. The latter variety here mentioned prevails in the inner patches growing in quiet waters. The former kind is common about outer reefs, since large areas in the coral plantation are mere sand. It is still more abundant, forming the bottom among the inner patches, or in the lagoons, where the finer detritus is washed by the sea. A glance at the chart of the Feejees or at the Kingsmills, (a copy of which, from Capt. Wilkes's Narrative is inserted in this volume,) will show how large a portion of the reef increases from these fine accumulations. The exterior of a coral island, for a few hundred yards, excepting some islets within, is the only part which is the proper growth of the living reef. Within the exterior reef the coral structure may consist almost wholly of the compact homogeneous white limestone we have described. The elevated island of Metia was for a long time after elevation exposed to the ravages of the sea, before the present shore-reefs accumulated to give it protection. Proofs of degradation along the coast have been referred to. There is much reason, therefore, for believing that the Metia now existing, exposes on its eastern and southern sides at least (where particularly examined by us) the interior of the original structure; and this view is supported by the compact character of the rock.

These reef-rocks receive also large contributions of sand or fragments from shells, which unite with the coral debris.

Besides the coral rocks formed beneath the waters surface, the beach or drift sands and gravel form stratified deposits of considerable extent, either bordering the shores within the range of the tides, or raised some distance above them. These drift-sand formations may cover the forming island and contribute largely to its progress; and sometimes they accumulate into drift hills forming when consolidated, hills of rock occasionally 60 or 80 feet in height. The rock is often loose and friable, but sometimes quite solid. The layers of the beach rock have a nearly constant dip of a few degrees, not exceeding eight, towards the water. The rock of the drift-hills or accumulations is more finely laminated, less firmly cemented, and dips whichever way the accumulating sandhill sloped, the layers being the successive sheets of sand which were drifted over it.

II. Coral reefs, though they may stretch along a coast for scores of miles, are seldom a single mile in width at the surface: and if elevated above the sea, they would stand as broad ramparts separated by passages mostly 20 to 200 feet deep, and often of great width. The substratum, however, is continuous coral-rock; and if these more elevated parts were removed by any process, after an elevation, they would leave an area of coral limestone often as extensive as the whole reef-grounds. This is at once seen from the figures of the Kingsmill chart and others on a preceding page. In an island like Deans's, one of the Paumotus, these reef-grounds are 1000 square miles in extent. It is true that the reefs at the surface gradually widen if the land is undergoing no subsidence. But when situated on a sloping bank, as usual, this widening gradually renders the bank steeper, and the rate of increase in width is rapidly diminished. And if the bank were not sloping, there is still reason to believe that the patches would not attain a great width at the surface of the sea, owing to the currents sweeping over them, occasioned partly by the position of a growing reef; and that therefore there would be unoccupied intervals or channels, as above alluded to, between the several reefs of a reef-ground.

The bearing of these facts upon the character and origin of ancient limestones, and the formation of channels, or valleys in such rocks, is apparent without particular explanation.

III. The occurrence of coral sand forming the exposed beaches, while the finer coral mud exists on the shores of the smaller lagoons, or at the bottom of the larger, affords an interesting illustration of the result produced by a triturating sea, as compared with that from more gently agitated waters. The rude seashore waves give rise to sand or pebbles; while the gentle undulations or ripplings of inland waters produce mud by their finer trituration. In the latter case the finely comminuted matter is retained beneath the quiet waters, in the former the rude action washes it away.

IV. The almost total absence of fossils from many parts of the coral reef-rock, and generally from the shore sandrocks, is one of the most striking facts here exemplified. These rocks are formed in the midst of life, and out of the enduring remains of animals; yet fossils, (as shown at Metia and other elevated reefs,) are often rare.

This absence of organic remains characterizes almost invariably the *drift* sandrock. On Oahu, where this rock forms hills thirty or forty feet in height above the reef-rock, not a fossil nor a fragment of one was distinguished by us, neither of shells nor corals. This fact had been previously remarked by some of the intelligent residents, and it was a matter of dispute whether one or two shells had not been found. These formations are but a few rods from waters prolific with the productions of the sea, and were made from them.

An explanation of this peculiarity, is obvious on the principle already discussed—the action of a triturating sea. Everything washed towards the shores, is ground down by this action and reduced to sand; and a large part of the sand is worn out and carried off by the sea; or, being thrown up by the reef, is blown inward by the winds.

It is a natural inference from these facts, that the non-fossiliferous sandstones of our continents are no good evidence of the absence or sparing diffusion of animal life in the seas about whose shores they may have been formed. If this destruction of fossils is so complete when the sands are of limestone, much more rapid and thorough should it be when they are siliceous. As the sea by its action bears off the finer material, and leaves only what is in the condition of sand or a coarser material, the lime of fossils might be almost wholly removed from among siliceous sands, and hardly a trace remain which the chemist could detect.

V. The formation of *chalk* from coral is known to be exemplified at only one spot among the reefs of the Pacific. The coral mud described appears to be a fit material for its production; and when dried it takes much the appearance of chalk. This fact was pointed out by Mr. Darwin, and was suggested to the writer by the mud in the lagoon of Honden Island. Still it does not explain the main point; for under all ordinary circumstances, this mud solidifies into compact limestone, instead of chalk. This appears, moreover, to be the result which should be expected. What condition then is necessary to vary the result, and set aside the ordinary process?

The bed of chalk referred to was not found on any of the coral islands, but in the elevated reef of Oahu, of which reef it formed a constituent part. It is twenty or thirty feet in extent, and eight or ten feet deep. The rock could not be distinguished from much of the chalk of England: it is equally fine and even in its texture, as earthy in its fracture, and so soft as to be used on the blackboard in the native schools. Some imbedded shells look precisely like chalk fossils. It consists, according to an analysis by Prof. B. Silliman, Jr., of

Carbonate of lime, . . .	92·800
Carbonate of magnesia, . .	2·385
Alumina, ...	0·250
Oxyd of iron, ...	0·543
Silica, ...	0·750
Phosphoric acid and fluorine, . .	2·113
Water and loss, . . .	1·148

The locality is situated on the shores just above high tide level, near the foot of Diamond Hill. This hill is an extinct tufa cone, near seven hundred feet in height, rising from the water's edge, and in its origin it must have been partly submarine. It is one of the lateral cones of eastern Oahu, and was thrown up at the time of an eruption through a fissure, the lavas of which appear at the base. There was some coral on the shores when the eruption took place, as is evident from imbedded fragments in the tufa; but the reef containing the chalk appeared to have been subsequent in formation. There is no certain proof yet ascertained of any connection between the fires of the mountain and the formation of the chalk.

The facts leave the subject of the origin of chalk still in uncertainty. Its fine earthy texture is evidence that the deposit was not subaerial seashore accumulation, as only sandstones and conglomerates, with rare instances of more compact rocks, are thus formed. Sandrock making is the peculiar prerogative, the world over, of shores exposed to waves, either marine or fresh water. We should infer, therefore, that the accumulations were produced either in confined areas, into which the fine material from a beach may have been washed, or on the shores of shallow, quiet seas: in other words, under the same conditions nearly as are required to produce the calcareous mud of the coral island. But, although the agency of fire in the result cannot be proved, it is by no means improbable, from the position of the bed of chalk, that there may have been a hot spring at the spot occupied by it. That there were some peculiar circumstances distinguishing this from other parts of the reefs, is evident; and this appears to be the only probable supposition. If this be admitted, the existence of an elevated temperature might be suggested for certain areas during the deposition of the chalk strata. It is well known that heated waters dissolve lime much less readily than cold; and this might be a reason for its inferior hardness and earthy texture. The character of the cretaceous deposits presents many interesting points bearing upon this subject; but a discussion of them would be out of place here, as our object is simply to state such inferences as the facts observed among existing reefs may have suggested.

This coral chalk has been examined microscopically by Professor Bailey, for infusoria and polythalamia, without detecting anything of this kind. It appeared to contain nothing organic.

VI. The analyses have shown that ordinary corals consist mainly of carbonate of lime. There is a small proportion of fluorids and phosphates, with some silica, alumina, and oxyd of iron. These fluorids and phosphates, existing in the coral, must exist also in the limestone rock made from coral. It is probable from some trials made by Prof. Silliman, Jr., that these constituents may be found also in many shells.

From the several analyses of corals by Mr. Silliman, we infer that the fluorids and phosphates amount, on an average, to about ¼th per cent., or 0·25 parts in a hundred of coral: and the amount in the same manner of the phosphates, is 0·05 per cent. A cubic foot of coral, as deduced from the average specific gravity, weighs one hundred and fifty-seven pounds, and consequently, in each cubic foot, there must be full six and one-fourth ounces of fluorids, and one and one-fourth ounces of phosphates: and in each cubic rod seventeen hundred pounds of fluorids, and three hundred and forty pounds of phosphates. These fluorids are fluorids of calcium and magnesium, and the phosphates, phosphates of lime and magnesia. To obtain the amount of these ingredients in a reef a mile long, half a mile wide and a hundred feet deep, the estimate for a cubic rod should be multiplied by 320,000; which will give for the fluorids more than five hundred millions of pounds.

Late geological researches have placed it beyond doubt that the various limestones consist mainly, like coral limestone, of animal remains, among which, in many instances, corals have a conspicuous place. These limestones often contain crystallizations of fluorid of calcium (fluor spar); and in other beds which have been acted upon by heat, and thus rendered crystalline, there are, besides this mineral, crystallizations of apatite, (phosphate of lime,) and chondrodite (consisting of fluorine, magnesia and silica). Moreover, these are among the most common minerals of such limestones. The above facts supply us with a full explanation of their origin. The fluorine, phosphoric acid, magnesia, and silica present, are adequate for all results, without looking to other sources for the elements of these disseminated minerals. Instead, therefore, of being extraneous minerals introduced into the limestone rock, they are (or may be in some instances) an essential part of its constitution. And they have been separated from the general mass by a segregation of like atoms, under well-known principles, while the rock was subjected to an elevated temperature. The fluorid of calcium appears to crystallize without much heat; but apatite and chondrodite are found mainly in *granular* limestones, which show, by their crystalline texture, that they have been subjected either to a very high temperature, or to one long continued of more moderate degree.

Lord Byron, of the Blonde, states that specimens of *phosphate of lime* (apatite,) were actually collected on Mauki, of the Hervey Group, one of the elevated coral islands.

VII. The cementation of coral sand along shores and beneath the sea is illustrated among all reefs, and is the process by which reef-rocks are formed. The sea-water receives some carbonate of lime into solution, and again deposits it among the deposited sand and fragments which lie compacted together. The same process takes place among the beach sands and the drift heaps. The eminences of drift sandrock at the Sandwich islands were covered in part by a smooth, solid crust, two or three lines thick, and made of layers like stalagmite, which was formed by the solution of lime from the surface by the rains, and its deposition again on evaporation.

The waters of the sea have been found to contain a small proportion of free carbonic acid, which is sufficient to enable it to dissolve the carbonate of lime of the corals.

Analyses of the coral limestone of the elevated coral island Matea, by Prof. B. Silliman, Jr., have determined the singular fact that although the corals themselves contain very little carbonate of magnesia, this salt is largely present in some specimens of the rock. The rock is hard (H. = 4·25), and splintery in fracture, with the specific gravity 2·690.

Carbonate of lime, . . .	61·93
Carbonate of magnesia, . .	38·07*

Another specimen from the same island, having the specific gravity 2·646, afforded 5·29 per cent. of carbonate of magnesia. The first was a compact, homogeneous specimen, and the other was partly fragmentary. Recent examinations of coral sand, and coral mud from the islands, give no different composition, as regards the magnesia, from that for corals. The coral sand from the straits of Balabac afforded carbonate of lime, 98·26, carbon-

* The *magnesia* in this analysis was directly determined, the lime being inferred from the loss.

ate of magnesia, 1·38, alumina, 0·24, phosphoric acid and silica, a trace.

We cannot account for this supply of magnesia except by referring to the magnesian salts of the ocean. It is an instance of dolomization, during the consolidation of the rock beneath sea-water, and throws light on this much vexed question.

This subject is illustrated, and the view we sustain confirmed, by an article on the formation of dolomite from carbonate of lime, published in the Naturwissenschaftliche Abhandlungen edited by W. Haidinger, (4to. Vienna, 1847.) According to von Morlot, in this paper, Haidinger has recently shown both by the frequent association of gypsum with dolomite, and by chemical experiment, that carbonate of lime and sulphate of magnesia, when together, undergo a double decomposition, the magnesia taking the place of part of the lime, and the excluded lime combining with the sulphuric acid set free. The result is *magnesian carbonate of lime*, (dolomite,) and *hydrous sulphate of lime*, (gypsum,) the latter being separated, and either continuing in solution or solidifying, according to the amount formed or the proportion in the water. Von Morlot gives figures of specimens from different localities in which gypsum and dolomite are intimately associated; and among them are some of fossil corals.

According to Haidinger, however, some heat is required for this result. Yet in the case of the coral rock and the *compact* magnesian limestones of our Western States, there is no evidence of the action of such heat; the subject therefore requires farther investigation.

The circumstance of a chemical change going on between the carbonate of lime and magnesian salt, (for such a change, under some circumstances, must have taken place,) is especially favorable for consolidation. When the coral is a fine mud, and the grains are therefore extremely fine, the dolomisation might extend to the grains themselves, as well as the infiltrating material acting as a cement. But when the grains of coral are large, or there are pebbles, the infiltrated material that might be magnesian would constitute but a small part of the whole bed. Hence it is obvious that such formations in cold waters should not always in the mass have the proportions of a true dolomite, (54·2 of carbonate of lime, to 45·8 of carbonate of magnesia;) they would probably attain such proportions under an ocean during that action of heat required alike for crystallization and chemical combination.*

* Prof. Horsford, in a paper on the consolidation of coral reef-rock, read before the last meeting of the American Association at Albany, (August, 1851), attributes this consolidation to the presence of organic matter which undergoes decomposition, as follows:—the sulphur present produces sulphuretted hydrogen; this changes to sulphuric acid, whence results sulphate of lime and a soluble carbonate of lime; then ammonia (resulting from the nitrogen) carries off the sulphuric acid as sulphate

VIII. It is an inquiry of some interest, whether, in an archipelago like the Paumotus, coral debris is not carried from the coral islands, and distributed over the bottom of the ocean; and whether limestones thus originating, are not in process of formation. I venture no positive assertion on this subject, yet would express strong doubts. The fact that soundings off some high islands, as we recede from the reef-growing depths, lose more and more in the proportion of coral sand, till we finally reach a bottom of basaltic earth, like the material of the island, bears against any such hypothesis. This was found to be the case off Upolu, where the reefs are extensive.

The action of the waves tends to throw back the material washed into the sea by fresh water streams and other currents, and in this manner extensive shore or shallow-water accumulations have been formed in all ages of the world. The formation from land debris of deep sea deposits, outside of soundings, is an hypothesis of geologists, yet to be proved. Such results may perhaps take place off the mouths of large rivers like the Amazon, the force of whose currents carries their transported material far to sea; but not, it would seem, in any case where the streams are small, or where the river current can not be traced out to sea much beyond soundings.

It remains still to speak of the proofs of elevation or subsidence presented by coral islands throughout the Pacific, and of the former extent of Pacific lands compared with the present. But these topics relating to the dynamics of the ocean, form a separate chapter.

We might dwell also on the formation of caverns by the rains becoming subterranean waters; on the illustration of the action of marine currents afforded by this subject; on the agency of polyps in rock-making. But the deductions are too obvious to require farther remark.

---

of ammonia and leaves the lime as a soluble hydrate, which remains united with the carbonate of lime, forming a compound like that indicated as existing in mortar by Fuchs; the final removal of the water by evaporation leaves the rock in a crystallized state. For a full statement of this author's views, see the American Journal of Science, [2], xiv, 245, and for a criticism on the same, ibid., p. 410.

CHAPTER V.

ON CHANGES OF LEVEL IN THE PACIFIC OCEAN.

EVIDENCES of change of level in the Pacific are to be looked for in the height or condition of the coral reef formations or deposits; in the character of the igneous rocks; and in the features of the surface. The points of evidence are as follows:—

A. Evidences of elevation.

1. *Patches of coral reef, or deposits of shells and sand from the reefs, above the level where they are at present forming.*

The coral reef-rock has been shown occasionally to increase by growth of coral, to a height of four to six inches above low tide level when the tide is but three feet, and to twice this height with a tide of six feet. It may, therefore, be stated as a general fact that the limit to which coral *may* grow above ordinary low tide, is about one-sixth the height of the tide, though it seldom attains this height.

Beach accumulations of large masses seldom exceed *eight* feet above high tide, and the finer fragments and sand may raise the deposit to ten feet. But with the wind and waves combined, or on prominent points where these agents may act from opposite directions, such accumulations may be *thirty* to *forty* feet in height. These are drift deposits, finely laminated, generally with a sandy texture, and commonly without a distinguishable fragment of coral or shell; and in most of these particulars they are distinct from reef-rocks. (See pages 17 and 32.)

2. *Sedimentary deposits, or layers of rolled stones interstratified among the igneous layers.*

3. *Compactness of the igneous rocks.*—The great uncertainty of this kind of evidence has been shown in another place.

B. Evidences of Subsidence.

1. *The existence of wide and deep channels between an island and any of its coral reefs;* or in other words, *the existence of barrier reefs.*

2. *Lagoon Islands or Atolls.*

3. *Submerged atolls.*

4. *Deep bay-indentations in coasts as the terminations of valleys.*—In the remarks upon the valleys of the Pacific Islands, it has been shown that they were in general formed by the waters of the land, unaided by the sea; that the sea tends only to level

off the coast, or give it an even outline. When therefore, we find the several valleys continued on beneath the sea, and their enclosing ridges standing out in long narrow points, there is reason to suspect that the island has subsided after the formation of its valleys. For such an island as Tahiti could not subside even a few scores of feet without changing the even outline into one of deep coves or bays, the ridges projecting out to sea on every side, like the spread legs of a spider. The absence of such coves, on the contrary, is evidence that any subsidence which has taken place, has been comparatively small in amount.

5. *Seashore alluvial flats or deposits.*

6. *The lava surface of a volcanic island, sloping without interruption beneath the water, instead of terminating in a shore cliff of a hundred feet or so.*

C. Probable evidence of subsidence now in progress.

1. *An atoll reef without green islets, or with but few small spots of verdure.*—The accumulation requisite to keep the reef at the surface-level, during a slow subsidence, renders it impossible for the reef to rise above the waves unless the subsidence is extremely slow.

From the above review of evidences of change of level, it appears that where there are no *barrier* reefs, and only fringing reefs, the corals afford no evidence of subsidence. But it does not follow that the existence of only fringing reefs, or of no reefs at all, is proof *against* a subsidence having taken place. For we have elsewhere shown that through volcanic action, and at times, other causes, corals may not have begun to grow till a recent period, and, therefore, we learn nothing from them as to what may previously have taken place. While, therefore, a distant barrier is evidence of change of level, we can draw no conclusion either one way or the other, as is done by Darwin, from the fact that the reefs are small or wholly wanting, until the possible operation of the several causes limiting their distribution has been duly considered.

The influence of volcanoes in preventing the growth of zoophytes, extends only so far as the submarine action may heat the water, and it may, therefore, be confined within a few miles of a volcanic island, or to certain parts only of its shores.

There are three epochs of changes in elevation which may be distinguished and separately considered. 1. The subsidence indicated by atolls and barrier reefs. 2. Elevations during more recent periods, and also during the same epoch of subsidence. 3. Changes of level anterior to the atoll subsidence and the growth of recent corals. On this last point, we have few facts.

1. *Subsidence indicated by atolls and barrier reefs.*

In a survey of the ocean, the eye observing its numerous atolls, sees in each, literally as well as poetically, a coral urn upon a rocky island that lies buried beneath the waves. Through the equatorial latitudes, such marks of subsidence abound, from the Eastern Paumotu to the Western Carolines, a distance of about six thousand geographical miles. In the Paumotu Archipelago there are about eighty of these atolls. Going westward, a little to the north of west, they are found to dot the ocean at irregular intervals; and at the Tarawan Group, the Carolines commence, which consist of seventy or eighty atolls.

If a line be drawn from Pitcairn's island, the southernmost of the Paumotus, by the Gambier Group, the north of the Society Group, Samoa, and the Salomon Islands to the Pelews, it will form nearly a straight boundary trending N. 70° W., running between the atolls on one side and the high islands of the Pacific on the other, the former lying to the North of the line, and the latter to the South.

Between this boundary line and the Hawaiian Islands, an area nearly two thousand miles wide and six thousand long, there are two hundred and four islands, of which *only three are high* exclusive of the eight Marquesas. These three are Ualan, Banabe (Ascension or Pounypet) and Hogoleu, all in the Caroline Archipelago. South of the same line, within three degrees of it, there is an occasional atoll; but beyond this distance, there are none excepting the few in the Friendly Group, and one or two in the Feejees.

If each coral island scattered over this wide area indicates a subsidence of an island, we may believe that the subsidence was general throughout the area. Moreover, each atoll, could we measure the thickness of the coral constituting it, would inform us nearly of the extent of the subsidence where it stands; for they are actually so many registers placed over the ocean, marking out not only the site of a buried island, but also the depth at which it lies covered. We have not the means of applying the evidence; but there are facts at hand, which may give at least comparative results.

a. We observe, *first*, that barrier reefs are, in general, evidence of less subsidence than atoll reefs. (p. 89.) Consequently the great preponderance of the former just below the southern boundary line of the coral island area, and farther south the entire absence of atolls, while atolls prevail so universally north of this line, are evidence of little depression just below the line; of less farther south; and of the greatest amount, north of the line or over the coral area.

b. The subsidence producing an atoll, when continued, gradually reduces it's size, until finally it becomes so small that the lagoon is obliterated ; and consequently a prevalence of these small islands is presumptive evidence of the greater subsidence. We observe, in application of this principle, that the coral islands about the equator, five or ten degrees south, between the Paumotus and the Tarawan Islands, are the smallest of the ocean : several of them are without lagoons, and some not a mile in diameter. At the same time, in the Paumotus, and among the Tarawan and Marshall Islands, there are atolls twenty to fifty miles in length, and rarely one less than three miles. It is probable, therefore, that the subsidence indicated was greatest at some distance north of the boundary line, over the region of small equatorial islands, between the meridian of 150° W. and 180°.

c. When after thus reducing the size of the atoll, the subsidence continues its progress, or when it is too rapid for the growing reef, it finally sinks the coral island, which, therefore, disappears from the ocean. Now it is a remarkable fact that while the islands about the equator above alluded to indicate greater subsidence than farther south, north of these islands, that is, between them and the Hawaiian Group, there is a wide blank of ocean without an island, which is near twenty degrees in breadth. This area lies between the Hawaiian, the Fanning and the Marshall islands, and stretches off between the first and last of these groups, far to the northwest.

Is it not then a legitimate conclusion that the subsidence which was least to the south beyond the boundary line, and increased northward, was still greater or more rapid over this open area; that the subsidence which reduced the size of the islands about the equator to mere patches of reef, was farther continued, and caused the total disappearance of islands that once existed over this part of the ocean?

d. That the subsidence gradually diminished southwestwardly from some point of greatest depression situated to the northward and eastward, is apparent from the Feejee Group alone. Its northeast portion, as the chart shows, consists of immense barriers, with barely a single point of rock remaining of the submerged land; while in the west and southwest there are basaltic islands of great magnitude. Again, along to the north side of the Vanikoro Group, the Salomon Islands, and New Ireland, there are coral atolls, though scarcely one to the south.

In view of this combination of evidence, we cannot doubt that the subsidence increased from the south to the northward or northeastward, and was greatest between the Samoan and Hawaiian Islands near the centre of the area destitute of islands, about longitude 170° to 175° W. and 8° to 10° N.

But we may derive some additional knowledge respecting this area of subsidence from other facts.

Hawaiian Range.—We observe that the western islands in the Hawaiian Range, beyond Bird Island, are coral islands, and all indicate some participation in this subsidence. To the eastward in the range, Kauai and Oahu have only fringing reefs, yet in some places these reefs are half a mile to three-fourths in width. They indicate a long period since they began to grow, which is borne out by the features of Kauai showing a long respite from volcanic action. We consequently detect proof of but little subsidence of the islands. Moreover, there are no deep bays: and, besides, Kauai has a gently sloping coast plain of great extent, with a steep shore acclivity of one to three hundred feet, all tending to prove the smallness of the subsidence. We should, therefore, conclude that these islands lie near the limits of the subsiding area, and that the change of level was greatest at the western extremity of the range beyond Kauai.

Marquesas.—The Marquesas are remarkable for their abrupt shores, often inaccessible cliffs, and deep bays. The absence of gentle slopes along the shores, their angular features, abrupt soundings close alongside the islands, and deep indentations, all bear evidence of subsidence to some extent; for their features are very similar to those which Kauai or Tahiti would present, if buried half its height in the sea, leaving only the sharper ridges and peaks out of water. They are situated but five degrees north of the Paumotus, where eighty islands or more have disappeared, including one at least fifty miles in length. There is sufficient evidence that they participated in the subsidence of the latter, but not to the same extent. They are nearly destitute of coral.

Gambier or Mangareva Group.—In the Southern limits of the Paumotu Archipelago, where, in accordance with the foregoing views, the least depression in that region should have taken place, there are actually, as we have stated, two high islands, *Pitcairn's* and *Gambier's*. There is evidence, however, in the extensive barrier about the *Gambier's* (see cut on page 91), that this subsidence, although less than farther north, was by no means of small amount. On page 19, we have estimated it at 1150 feet. These islands, therefore, although towards the limits of the subsiding area, were still far within it. The valley-bays of the Mangareva islets are of great depth, and afford additional evidence of the subsidence.

Tahitian Islands.—The Tahitian Islands, along with Samoa and the Feejees, are near the southern limits of the area pointed out. Twenty-five miles to the north of Tahiti, within sight from its peaks, lies the coral island Tetuaroa, a register of subsidence. Tahiti itself, by its barrier reefs, gives evidence of the same kind of change; amounting, however, as we have estimated, to a depression of but two hundred and fifty or three hundred feet. The northwestern islands of the group lie more within the coral area, and correspondingly, they have wider reefs and channels, and deep bays, indicating a greater amount of subsidence.

Samoa.—The island of Upolu has extensive reefs, which, in many parts, are three-fourths of a mile wide, but no inner channel. We have estimated the subsidence at one or two hundred feet. The volcanic land west of Apia declines with an unbroken gradual slope of one to three degrees beneath the sea. The absence of a low cliff is probable evidence of a depression, as has been elsewhere shown. The island of Tutuila has abrupt shores, deep bays and little coral. It appears probable, therefore, that it has experienced a greater subsidence than Upolu. Yet the central part of Upolu has very similar bays on the north, which would afford apparently the same evidence; and it is quite possible that the facts indicate a sinking which either preceded the ejections that now cover the eastern and western extremities of Upolu, or accompanied this change of level. Savaii has small reefs, from which we gather no certain facts bearing on this subject. East of Tutuila is the coral island, Rose. It may be therefore, that the greatest subsidence in the group was at its eastern extremity.

Feejee Islands.—We have already remarked upon this group. A large amount of subsidence is indicated by the reefs in every portion of the group, but it was greatest beyond doubt in the northeastern part.

Ladrones.—The Ladrones appear to have undergone their greatest subsidence at the north extremity of the range, the part nearest the centre of the coral area: for although the fires at the north have continued longest to burn, the islands are the smallest of the group, the whole having disappeared except the summits, which still eject cinders. The southern islands of the group have wide reefs, but they afford no good evidence of any great extent of subsidence since the reefs began to form.

We have thus fo..owed around the borders of the coral area: and besides proving the reality of the limits, have ascertained some facts with reference to a gradual diminution of the subsidence towards and beyond these limits. A line from Pitcairns to Bird in the Hawaiian Group appears to have a corresponding position on the northeast with the southern boundary line of the coral area; the two include a large triangular area. An axis nearly bisecting this triangular space, drawn from Pitcairns towards Japan, actually passes through the region of greatest subsidence, as we have before determined it, and may be considered the *axial line* or *line of greatest depression* for the great area of subsidence.

It is worthy of special note, *that this axial line or line of greatest depression coincides in direction with the mean trend of the great ranges of islands, it having the course* N. 52° W.

The southern boundary line of the coral area, as we have laid it down, lies within the area of subsidence, although near its limits. There are places along this line where this area has been prolonged farther than elsewhere. One of these regions lies between Samoa and Rotuma, and extends down to the Feejees and Tonga Group; another is east of Samoa, reaching towards the Hervey Group. Each of these extensions trends parallel with the groups of islands; and with the part of the line east of Tahiti. It would seem, therefore, that the Society and Samoa islands were regions of less change of level than the deep seas about them.

What may be the Extent of the Coral Subsidence?—It is very evident that the sinking of the Society, Samoan, and Hawaiian Islands has been small compared with that required to submerge all the lands on which the Paumotus and the other Pacific atolls rest. One, two, or five hundred feet could not have buried all the many peaks of these islands. Even the 1500 feet of depression at the Gambier Group is shown to be at a distance from the axis of the subsiding area. The groups of high islands above mentioned contain summits from 4000 to 14,000 feet above the sea; and can we believe it possible that throughout this large area, when the two hundred islands now sunk were above the waves, there were none equal in altitude to the mean of these heights? That all should have been within nine thousand feet in elevation, is by no means probable. However moderate our estimate, there must still be allowed a sinking of several thousand feet: and however much we increase it within probable bounds, we shall not arrive at a more surprising change of level than our continents show that they have undergone.

Between the New Hebrides and Australia the reefs and islands mark out another area of depression, which may have been simultaneously in progress. The long reef of one hundred and fifty miles from the north cape of New Caledonia and the wide barrier on the west cannot be explained without supposing a subsidence of one or two thousand feet at the least. The distant barrier of New Holland is proof of as great if not greater subsidence.

Effect of the Subsidence.—The facts surveyed give us a long insight into the past, and exhibit to us the Pacific scattered over with lofty lands where there are now only humble monumental atolls. Had there been no growing coral, the whole would have passed without a record. These permanent registers, planted ages past in various parts of the tropics, exhibit in enduring characters the oscillations which the "stable" earth has since undergone. Thus Divine wisdom creates and makes the creations inscribe their own history; and there is a noble pleasure in deciphering even one sentence in this Book of Nature.

From the actual extent of the coral reefs and islands, we know that the whole amount of high land lost to the Pacific by the subsidence, was at least fifty thousand square miles. But since atolls are necessarily smaller than the land they cover, and the more so, the farther subsidence has proceeded;—since many lands from their abrupt shores, or through volcanic agency must have had no reefs about them, and have disappeared without a mark; and others may have subsided too rapidly for the corals to retain themselves at the surface; it is obvious that this estimate is far below the truth. It is apparent that in many cases, islands now disjoined, have been once connected, and thus several atolls may have been made about the heights of a single subsiding land of large size. Such facts show farther error in the above estimate, evincing that the scattered atolls and reefs do not tell half the story. Why is it, also, that the Pacific islands are confined to the tropics, if not that beyond thirty degrees the zoophyte could not plant its growing registers?

Yet we should beware of hastening to the conclusion that a continent once occupied the place of the ocean, or a large part of it, which is without proof. To establish the former existence of a Pacific continent is an easy matter for the fancy; but geology knows nothing of it, nor even of its probability.

The island of Banabe in the Caroline archipelago affords evidence of a subsidence *in progress*, as my friend, Mr. Horatio Hale, the Philologist of the Expedition, gathered from a foreigner who had been for a while a resident on this island. Mr. Hale remarks, after explaining the character of certain sacred structures of stone: "It seems evident that the constructions at Ualan and Banabe are of the same kind, and were built for the same purpose. It is also clear that when the latter were raised, the islet on which they stand was in a different condition from what it now is. For at present they are actually in the water; what were once paths, are now passages for canoes, and as O'Connell [his informant] says, 'when the walls are broken down the water enters the inclosures.'" Mr. Hale hence infers "that the land, or the whole group of Banabe, and perhaps all the neighboring groups, have undergone a slight depression." He also states respecting a small islet near Ualan, "From the description given of Leilei, a change of level of one or two feet would render it uninhabitable, and reduce it, in a short time, to the same state as the isle of ruins at Banabe."

Period of the subsidence.—The period during which these changes were in progress, was probably since the tertiary epoch. In the island of Metia, elevated over two hundred feet, the corals below were the same as those now existing, as far as we could judge from the fossilized specimens. At the inner margin of shore reefs, there is the same identity with existing genera. We do not claim to have examined the basement of the coral islands, and offer these facts as the only evidence on this point that is within reach. We cannot know with absolute certainty that the present races of zoophytes may not be the successors of others of the secondary epoch: but we do know that we have little reason in facts observed for even the suspicion. For a long time volcanic action was too general and constant for the growth of corals: and this may have continued to interfere till a comparatively late period, if we may judge from the appearance of the rocks, even on Tahiti.

The evidence of subsidence from coral islands might be pursued to other regions in other seas; but we here only refer to the facts on this point presented in our review of the geographical distribution of corals, since we cannot speak from personal observation.

The subsidence has probably for a considerable period ceased in most if not all parts of the ocean, and subsequent elevations of many islands and groups have taken place which we shall soon consider. In some of the Northern Carolines, the Pescadores, and perhaps some of the Marshall Islands, the proportion of dry land is so very small compared with the great extent of the atoll, that there is reason to suspect a slow sinking even at the present time: and it is a fact of special interest in connection with it that this region is near the axial line of greatest depression, where, if in any part, the action should be longest continued.

Among the Kingsmills and Paumotus there is no reason whatever for supposing that a general subsidence is still in progress; the changes indicated are of a contrary character.

The results to which we have here been led obviously differ in many particulars from the deductions of Mr. Darwin.

2. *Elevations of Modern Eras in the Pacific.*

Since the period of subsidence, the history of which has occupied us in the preceding pages, there has been no equally general elevation. Yet various parts of the ocean bear evidence of changes confined to particular islands or groups of islands. While the former exemplify one of the grander events in the earth's history, in which a large segment of the globe was concerned, the latter exhibit its minor changes over limited areas. The instances of these changes are so numerous and so widely scattered, that they convince us of a cessation in the previous general subsidence.

The most convenient mode of reviewing the subject is to state in order, the facts relating to each group.

a. Paumotu Archipelago.—The islands of this archipelago appear in general to have that height which the ocean may give to the materials. Nothing was detected which satisfied us of any *general* elevation in progress through the archipelago. The large extent of wooded land shows only that the islands have been long at their present level: and on this point our own observations confirm those of Mr. Darwin. There are examples of elevation in particular islands however, some of which are of unusual interest. The instances examined by the Expedition, were Honden (or Henuake), Dean's Island (or Nairsa), Aurora (or Metia), and Clermont Tonnerre. Beside these, Elizabeth Island has been described by Beechey, and the same author mentions certain facts relating to Ducie's Island and Osnaburgh, which afford some suspicions of a rise.

Honden or Dog Island.—This island is wooded on its different sides, and has a shallow lagoon. The beach is eight feet high and the land about eleven. There are three entrances to the lagoons, all of which were dry at low water, and one only was filled at high water. Around the lagoon, near the level of high tide, there were numerous shells of Tridacna lying in cavities in the coral rock, precisely as they occur alive on the shore reef. As these Tridacnas evidently lived where the shells remain, and do not occur alive more than six or eight inches, or a foot at the most, above low tide, they prove, in connection with the other facts, an elevation of *twenty inches* or *two feet.*

Nairsa or Dean's Island.—The south side of Dean's island, the largest of the Paumotus, was coasted along by the Peacock, and from the vessel we observed that the rim of land consisted for miles of an even wall of coral rock, apparently six or eight feet above high tide. This wall was broken into rude columns, or excavated with arches and caverns; in some places the sea had carried it away from fifty to one hundred rods and then there followed again a line of columns and walls, with occasional arches as before. The reef, formerly lying at the level of low tide, had been raised above the sea, and subsequently had undergone degradation from the waves. The standing columns had some resemblance in certain parts to the masses seen here and there on the shore platforms of other islands; but the latter are only distantly scattered masses, while on this island, for the greater part of the course, there were long walls of reef-rock. The height moreover was greater, and they occurred too on the *leeward* side of the island, ranging along nearly its whole course.

The elevation here indicated was at least *six feet;* but it may have been larger, as the observations were made from ship-board. Thirty miles to the southward of Dean's Island, we came to Metia, one of the most remarkable examples of elevation in the Pacific.

Metia.—This island has already been described, and its elevation stated at *two hundred and fifty feet.* (See page 35.)

*Clermont Tonnerre,** according to Mr. Couthouy, shows the same evidence of elevation from Tridacnas as Honden Island. Clermont Tonnerre and Honden are in the northeastern limits of the Paumotus.

Elizabeth Island was early shown to be an elevated coral island by Beechey. This distinguished voyager represents it as having perpendicular cliffs fifty feet in height. From his description, it is obviously of the same character as Metia; the elevation is *eighty* feet.

Ducie's Island is described by Beechey as twelve feet high, which would indicate an elevation of at least *one* or *two* feet.

Osnaburgh Island, according to the same author, affords evidence of having increased its height since the wreck of the Matilda in 1792. He contrasts the change from "a reef of rocks," as reported by the crew, to "a conspicuously wooded island," the condition when he visited it; and states further, that the anchor, iron-works, and a large gun (4-pounder) of this vessel were two hundred yards inside of the line of breakers. Captain Beechey suggests that the coral had grown, and thus increased the height. But this process might have buried the anchor if the reef were covered with growing corals, (which is improbable,) and could not have raised its level. If there has been any increase of height, (which we do not say is certain,) it must have arisen from subterranean action.

b. Tahitian Group.—The island of Tahiti presented us no conclusive evidence of elevation. The shore plains are said to rest on coral, which the mountain debris has covered; but they do not appear to indicate a rise of the land. The descriptions by different authors of the other islands of this group, do not give sufficient reason for confidently believing that any of them have been elevated. The change, however, of the barrier reef around Bolabola into a verdant islet encircling the island, may be evidence that a long period has elapsed since the subsidence ceased; and as such a change is not common in the Pacific, we may suspect that it has been furthered by at least a small amount of elevation. The observation by the Rev. D. Tyerman with regard to the shells found at Huahine high above the sea, may be proof of elevation; but the earlier erroneous conclusions with regard to Tahiti, teach us to be cautious in admitting it without a more particular examination of the deposit.

c. Hervey and Rurutu Groups.—These groups lie to the southwest and south of Tahiti.

* This island was not visited by the writer, as only the officers of the Vincennes attempted to land on it.

Atiu (Wateoo of Cook) is a raised coral island. Cook observes that it is "nearly like Mangaia." The land near the sea is only a bank of coral ten or twelve feet high, and steep and rugged. The surface of the island is covered with verdant hills and plains, with no streams.*

Mauke is a low elevated coral island.†

Mitiaro resembles Mauke.‡

Okatutaia is a low coral island, not more than six or seven feet high above the beach, which is coral sand. It has a light-reddish soil.

Mangaia is girted by an elevated coral reef *three hundred* feet in height. Mr. Williams speaks of it as coral, with a small quantity of fine-grained basalt in the interior of the island; he states again that a broad ridge (the reef) girts the hills.§

Rurutu has an elevated coral reef *one hundred and fifty* feet in height.‖

With regard to the other islands of these groups, *Manuai*, *Aitutaki*, *Rarotonga*, *Rimetara*, *Tubuai*, and *Raivavai*, the descriptions by Williams and Ellis appear to show that they have undergone no recent elevation.

d. Scattered Islands in the latitudes between the Society and Samoan Groups.—These coral islands, as far as we can ascertain, are low like the Paumotus, excepting some of the Fanning Group north of the equator, and possibly Jarvis and Malden.

Of the *Fanning Group*, (situated near the equator, south of the Hawaiian Group,)

Washington Island is three miles in diameter, without a proper lagoon; the whole surface, as seen by us, was covered densely with cocoanut trees. This unusual size for an island without a lagoon indicates an elevation, which the height of the island, estimated at twelve feet, confirms. The elevation may have been *two* or *three* feet.

Palmyra Island, just northwest of Washington, is described by Fanning as having two lagoons; the westernmost contains twenty fathoms water. *Fanning's Island*, to the southeast of Washington, is described by the same voyager as lower than that island. The accounts give no evidence of elevation.

---

* Cook's Voyage, vol. i, pp. 180, 197. Williams's Miss. Enterprises, i, 47, 48, first Am. edit., Appleton.

† Williams's Miss. Ent., pp. 39, 47, 264.

‡ Ibid. pp. 39, 264.

§ Williams's Miss. Ent., pp. 48, 50, 249. See also Mr. Darwin, p. 132.

‖ Williams's Miss. Ent., p. 50.—Stutchbury describes the coral rock as one hundred and fifty feet high. West of England Journal, i.—Tyerman and Bennet describe the island as having a high central peak with lower eminences, and speak of the coral rock as two hundred feet high on one side of the bay and three hundred on the other (ii, 102).—Ellis says that the rocks of the interior are in part basaltic, and in part vesicular lava, iii, 393.

Christmas Island, still farther to the southeast, according to the description of Cook, its discoverer, had the rim of land in some parts three miles wide. He mentions narrow ridges lying parallel with the sea-coast, which "must have been thrown up by the sea, though it does not reach within a mile of some of these places." The proof of a small elevation is decided, but its amount cannot be determined from the description. The account of F. D. Bennett, (Geographical Jour., vii, 226,) represents it as a low coral island.

Jarvis Island, as seen from the Peacock, appeared to be eighteen or twenty feet in height, which, if not exaggerated by refraction, (we think it not probable,) would show an elevation of six or eight feet. This island is a sand flat, with little vegetation, and is but two hundred miles south of Christmas Island.

Malden, two hundred and fifty miles southeast of Jarvis, near latitude 4° S. and longitude 155° W., visited by Lord Byron, is described as not over forty feet high; but this may be the whole height, including the height of the trees.

e. Tonga Islands and others in their vicinity.

All the islands of the Tonga group about which there are reefs, give evidence of elevation: *Tongatabu* and the *Hapai* islands consist solely of coral, and are elevated atolls.

Eua, at the south extremity of the line, has an undulated, mostly grassy surface, in some parts eight hundred feet in height. Around the shores, as was seen by us from shipboard, there is an elevated layer of coral reef-rock, twenty feet thick, worn out into caverns, and with many spout-holes. Between the southern shores and the highest part of the island, we observed three distinct terraces. Coral is said to occur at a height of three hundred feet. From the appearance of the land, we judged that the interior was basaltic; but nothing positive was ascertained with regard to it.

Tongatabu (an island visited by us) lies near Eua, and is in some parts fifty or sixty feet high, though in general but twenty feet. It has a shallow lagoon, into which there are two entrances; some hummocks of coral reef-rock stand eight feet out of water.

Namuka and most of the *Hapaii* cluster, are stated by Cook to have abrupt limestone shores, ten to twenty feet in height. Namuka has a lagoon or salt lake at centre one and a half miles broad; and there is a coral rock in one part twenty-five feet high.*

Vavau, the northern of the Group, according to Williams, is a cluster of elevated islands of coral limestone, thirty to one hundred feet in height, having precipitous cliffs, with many excavations along the coast.†

* Cook's Voyage.—Williams, p. 296.

† Williams, p. 427.

Pylstaart's Island, south of Tongatabu, is a small rocky islet without coral. Tafua and Proby are volcanic cones, and the former is still active.

Savage Island, a little to the east of the Tonga Group, resembles Vavau in its coral constitution and cavernous cliffs. It is elevated *one hundred feet.**

Beveridge Reef, a hundred miles southeast of Savage, is low coral.

f. Samoan Islands.—No satisfactory evidences of elevation were detected about these islands.

g. Scattered Islands, north of Samoa.

These islands are all of coral, and several indicate an elevation of one to six feet. On account of the high tides, (4 to 6 feet,) the sea may give a height of ten or twelve feet to the land.

Swain's, near latitude 11° S., is fifteen to eighteen feet above the sea, where highest, and the beach is ten to twelve feet high. It is a small island, with a depression at centre, but no lagoon. The height proves an elevation of *three to six* feet.

Fakaafo, ninety miles to the north, is fifteen feet high. The coral reef-rock is raised in some places three feet above the present level of the platform. Elevation at least *three* feet.

Nukunono, or Duke of Clarence, near Fakaafo, was seen only from shipboard.

Oatafu, or Duke of York's, is in some parts fourteen feet high. Elevation *two* or *three* feet.

Enderby's and *Birnie's*, still farther north, are twelve feet high. Judging from the double slope of the beach on Enderby, this island may have undergone an elevation of *two* feet, the height of the upper slope; yet we think it doubtful.

Gardner's, *Hull*, *Sydney* and *Newmarket* were visited by the Expedition, but no satisfactory evidences of elevation on the first three were observed. The last is stated by Captain Wilkes to be *twenty-five* feet in height.

h. Feejee Islands.—The proofs of an elevation of four to six feet about the larger Feejee Islands, Viti Lebu and Vanua Lebu, and also Ovalau, are given in our report on this group. How far this rise affected other parts of the group, I have been unable definitely to determine: but as the extensive barrier reefs in the eastern part of the group, rarely support a green islet, they rather indicate a subsidence in those parts than an elevation.

i. Islands north of the Feejees.—Horne Island, Wallis, Ellice, Depeyster, and four islands on the track towards the Kingsmills, were passed by the Peacock; but from the vessel, no evidences of elevation could be distinguished. The first two are high

* Williams, pp. 275, 276. Foster estimates the height at fifty feet, and speaks of a depression about the centre.

islands, with barriers, and the others are low coral. *Rotuma*, (177° 15′ E., and 12° 30′ N.,) is another high island, to the west of Wallis's. It has encircling reefs, but we know nothing as to its changes of level.

k. Sandwich Islands.—Oahu affords decided proof of an elevation of twenty-five or thirty feet. There is an impression at Honolulu, derived from a supposed increasing height in the reef off the harbor, that the island is slowly rising. Upon this point I can offer nothing decisive. The present height of the reef is not sufficiently above the level to which it might be raised by the tides, to render it certain, from this kind of evidence, that the suspected elevation is in progress.

Kauai presents us with no evidence that the island, at the present time, is at a higher level than when the coral reefs begun: or at the most, no elevation is indicated beyond a foot or two. The drift sand rock of Koloa appears to be a proof of elevation, from its resemblance to those of Northern Oahu: but if so, there must have been a subsidence since, as it now forms a cliff on the shore that is gradually wearing away.

Molokai, according to information from the Rev. Mr. Andrews, has coral upon its declivities three hundred feet above the sea. The same gentleman informed us that on the western peninsula of *Maui*, coral occurs in some places eight hundred feet above the sea; and specimens of well defined coral were obtained at a height of five hundred feet. These islands were not visited by the writer.

With regard to *Molokai*, Mr. Andrews informed the author that the coral occurs "upon the acclivity of the eastern or highest part of the island, over a surface of more than twenty or thirty acres, and extends almost to the sea. We had no means of accurately measuring the height; but the specimens were obtained at least three hundred feet above the level of the sea, and probably four hundred. The specimens have distinctly the structure of coral. The distance from the sea was two to three miles."

Mr. Andrews, who appears to doubt the connection of the supposed coral on *Maui* with reefs, writes to the author as follows: "In no case have I seen the coral in a rocky ledge; it is generally mixed with the lava rock, to which it adheres. It has usually the appearance of burnt lime; and thus, large stones and rocks seem as though they had been whitewashed several times over, and sometimes it amounts to an inch in thickness, or an inch and a half. At other times the whitewash has found its way into cracks in the stones. Sometimes only one side of a stone is whitened by it, or only a corner of it. It is sometimes soft and crumbly, and at other times quite hard; and again it is mixed with the earth." From this description it appears to resemble the lime incrustations and seams of Diamond Hill, Punchbowl and Koko Head, Oahu, which occur at the same height, but most certainly give no evidence of elevation, as they have proceeded beyond doubt from aqueous eruptions carrying lime in solution. Fragments of coral, it will be remembered, occur in the tufa of these hills. This evidence from Maui, should therefore be received with great hesitation until farther examined.

Besides the above, there are large masses of coral rock, according to Mr. Andrews, along the shores of Maui, from *two* to *twelve* feet above high water. From his descriptions, this rock appears to be the reef-rock, like the raised reef of Oahu, and is probably proof of an elevation of at least *twelve* feet.

l. Kingsmill or Tarawan Group. (Plate I.)

Taputeouea or Drummond.—This is the southern island of the group. The reef rock near the village of Utiroa is a foot above low tide level, and consists of large massive Astreas and Meandrinas. The tide in the Kingsmill seas is seven feet; and consequently this evidence of a rise might be doubted, as some corals may grow to this height where the tide is so high. But these Astreas and Meandrinas, as far as observed by the writer, are not among the species that may undergo exposure at low tide, except it be to the amount of three or four inches; and it is probable that an elevation of at least *ten* or *twelve* inches has taken place.

Apia or *Charlotte's* Island, one of the northernmost of the group, has the *reef-rock* in some parts raised bodily to a height of six or seven feet above low water level, evidencing this amount of elevation. This elevated reef was observed for long distances between the several wooded islets; it resembled the south reef of Nairsa in the Paumotu Archipelago in its bare, even top, and bluff worn front. An islet of the atoll, where we landed, was twelve feet high, and the coral *reef-rock* was five or six feet above middle tide. A wall of this rock, having the same height extends along the reef from the islet. There was no doubt that it was due to an actual uplifting of the reef to a height of full *six* feet.

Nanouki, *Kuria*, *Maiana* and *Tarawa* lying between the two islands above mentioned, were seen only from the ship, and nothing decisive bearing on the subject of elevation was observed. On the northeast side of Nanouki there was a hill twenty or thirty feet in height covered with trees; but we had no means of learning that it was not artificial. We were, however, informed by Kirby, a sailor taken from Kuria, that the reef of *Apamama* was elevated precisely like that of Apia, to a height of *five* feet; and this was confirmed by Lieutenant Dehaven, who was engaged in the survey of the reef. We were told, also, that Kuria and Nanouki were similar in having the reef elevated though to a less extent. It would hence appear that the elevations in the group increase to the northward.

Maraki, to the north of Apia, is wooded throughout. We sailed around it without landing, and can only say that it has probably been uplifted like the islands south. *Makin*, the northernmost island, presented in the distant view no certain evidence of elevation.

The elevation of the Kingsmills accounts for the long continuity of the wooded lines of land, an unusual fact considering the size of the islands. The amount of fresh water obtained from springs is also uncommon. (p. 43.) The wear from storms would also be greater on islands which have been elevated.

m. Radack, Ralick and Caroline Islands.—No evidences of elevation in these groups are yet known. The very small amount of wooded land on the Pescadores inclines us to suspect rather a subsidence than an elevation; and the same fact might be gathered with regard to some of the islands south, from the charts of Kotzebue and Kruesenstern.

n. Ladrones.—The seventeen islands which constitute this group, may all have undergone elevations within a recent period, but owing to the absence of coral from the northern, we have evidence only with regard to the more southern.

Guam, according to Quoy and Gaymard, has coral rock upon its hills more than *six hundred* feet (one hundred toises) above the sea.

Rota, the next island north, afforded these authors similar facts, indicating the same amount of elevation.

o. Pelews and neighboring Islands.—The island *Feis*, three hundred miles southwest of Guam, is stated by Darwin, on the authority of Lutke, to be of coral, and *ninety* feet high. *Mackenzie* Island, seventy-five miles south of Feis, is a low atoll, as ascertained by the Expedition. No evidences of elevation are known to occur at the Pelews.

Melanesian Islands.—Among the New Hebrides, New Caledonia, Salomon Islands, the evidences of elevation have not yet been examined.

The details given on the preceding pages are here presented in a tabular form.

		FEET.
Paumotu Archipelago, ...	Honden, ...	$1\frac{1}{2}$ or 2
" "	Clermont Tonnere, ...	2
" "	Nairsa or Deans's, ...	6
" "	Elizabeth, ...	80
" "	Metia or Aurora, ...	250
" "	Ducie's, ...	1 or 2
Tahitian Group, ...	Tahiti, ...	0 ?
" "	Bolabola, ...	?

		FEET.
Hervey and Rurutu Groups,	Atiu,	12 ?
" " " "	Mauke,	somewhat elevated.
" " " "	Mitiaro,	" "
" " " "	Mangaia,	300
" " " "	Rurutu,	150
" " " "	Remaining Islands,	0 ?
North of the Tahitian,	Washington Island,	2 or 3
" " " "	Christmas,	2 ?
" " " "	Malden,	?
" " " "	Jarvis,	6 or 8 ?
Tongan Group,	Eua,	300 ?
" "	Tongatabu,	60
" "	Namuka and the Hapai,	25
" "	Vavau,	100
Savage Island,		100
Samoan Islands,		0
North of Samoa,	Swain's,	3 to 6
" " "	Fakaafo, or Bowditch,	3
" " "	Oatafu, or Duke of York's,	2 or 3
" " "	Enderby's,	2 ?
" " "	Gardner, Hull, Sidney, Newmarket,	0 ?
Feejee Islands,	Viti Levu and Vanua Levu, Ovalau,	5 or 6
	Eastern Islands,	0 ?
North of Feejees,	Horne, Wallis, Ellice, Depeyster,	0 ?
Sandwich Islands,	Kauai,	1 or 2
" "	Oahu,	25 or 30
" "	Molokai,	300
" "	Maui,	12—
Tarawan Islands,	Taputeouea,	1 or 2
" "	Nanouki, Kuria, Maiana and Tarawa,	2 or more.
" "	Apamama,	5
" "	Apia or Charlotte,	6 or 7
" "	Maraki,	2 or 3
" "	Makin,	0
Carolines,		none ascertained
Ladrones,	Guam,	600
"	Rota,	600
Feis,		90
Pelews,		0 ?
New Hebrides, New Caledonia,	Salomon Islands,	none ascertained.

Several deductions are at once obvious:—

1. That the elevations have taken place in all parts of the ocean.
2. That they have in some instances affected single islands, and not those adjoining.
3. That the amount is often very unequal in adjacent islands.
4. That in a few instances the change has been experienced by a whole group or chain of islands. The Tarawan Group is an instance, and the rise appears to increase from the southernmost island to Apia, and then to diminish again to the other extremity.

The Feejees may be an example of a rise at the west side of a group, and possibly a subsidence on the east; while a little farther east, the Tonga Islands constitute another extended area of elevation. We observe that while the Samoan Islands afford no evidences of elevation, the Tonga Islands on the south have been raised, and also the Fakaafo Group and others on the north.

We cannot, therefore, distinguish any evidence that a general rise is or has been in progress; yet some large areas appear to have been simultaneously affected, although the action has often been isolated. Metia and Elizabeth Island may have risen abruptly: but the changes of level in the Feejees and the Friendly Islands, appear to have taken place by a gradual action.

3. *Changes of Level in the Pacific preceding the Coral Reefs.*

The evidences of change of level previous to the growth of coral are to be looked for in the topographical features of the high islands, and the occurrence of conglomerate layers of rolled stones in the structure of the mountains.

To arrive at any general results on this subject, requires, therefore, a thorough knowledge of the surface of the islands, as well as their interior structure: and as regards the last mentioned point, the soil and vegetation over these tropical lands is everywhere an obstacle in the way of investigation. Our own surveys have led to few results, and these can be stated in a single paragraph.

In our account of the island of Oahu, we have mentioned the occurrence of layers of rounded stones and earth interstratified with finer material at Ewa, and occurring at a height of sixty feet above the sea. We were informed of similar deposits up a valley on this part of the island, at a much greater elevation, but did not have an opportunity to examine them. In crossing the mountains of the western peninsula of Maui, Dr. Pickering observed a basaltic pudding-stone, or conglomerate of half-rounded stones, two thousand feet above the level of the sea. On Mount Kea, similar beds were met with by Dr. Pickering at a height of six thousand feet. On the island of Tahiti a coarse conglomerate of partially rolled fragments was observed by the writer up a branch from the Matavai valley, at an elevation of about one thousand five hundred feet above the sea. From these facts, and others similar in the Feejees and Samoa, we may infer that many of the islands were at a lower level during some portion of their early history, while their formation was in progress. But they do not prove their submarine origin, nor anything definite respecting the actual condition of the seas. This remains for future exploration. The compact rocks of the interior of the islands, and especially the crystalline syenitic rocks of Tahiti, were at one time considered by the author evidence of their eruption beneath the pressure of an ocean; but this is not satisfactory, since the pressure required for compactness would be afforded in the interior of a volcano, by the molten lava itself.

From the surface of Mount Loa we learn that the occurrence of beds of lava with ropy lines characterizing the surface (produced by the flowing of the lava) indicates a subaerial origin. In ejections beneath the sea, the surface of the lava is so acted upon by the cold water that such lines are not preserved. From these indications we ascertain that Tahiti, Upolu, Savaii, Oahu, Maui, and Kauai were nearly at their present height when the *latest* eruptions took place.

We learn again from Mount Loa, that a subaerial origin is shown by a great number of lateral cones of lava or cinders. The absence of these small cones from Tahiti cannot, however prove the contrary; since the island has been subject to extensive denudation, and these minor craters would be the first parts to disappear. Western Maui, as well as the larger part of Kauai, resembles Tahiti. On Eastern Maui and Savaii these lateral cones are still numerous, and the surface of these lands bears evidence of recent subaerial fires, and little denudation.

The cavernous nature of Mount Loa, is another point that may be looked upon as proof of subaerial origin; and it is conclusive upon this point, as far as regards the exterior coating of Mount Loa, the only part exposed to view. Like the two preceding kinds of evidence, it is of very difficult application. In Eastern Oahu, however, in the lower slopes beyond Diamond Hill, there are many caverns so similar to those of Mount Loa, that they clearly evince that the land was above water when the ejections took place.

The recent ejected rocks of Mount Loa, though often very compact, still contain some ragged cellules; and this kind of cellule rather than the absence of them altogether is a good proof of the rocks cooling without pressure above. The application of this test leads us to no different results from those already stated.

We arrive, therefore, at the conclusion that while it is apparent that the latest eruptions of many of the Pacific islands were subaerial, and the most of these lands were at a much lower level in the course of their progress, we cannot point out which were of submarine origin; and of course we learn nothing with regard to the earliest condition of these centres of eruption, from examining the rocks above the present sea level.

The action of the sea on the cliffs of the islands before these shores were protected by reefs, is another source of evidence with regard to the level of the land at an early epoch. Such facts are very difficult to be identified; and we have distinguished only a single undoubted case. This occurs on the north side of Vanua Lebu, one of the Feejees.

The island of Mali upon this coast is, in fact, two islands: they are separated by a narrow passage, and stand but a short distance from the shore. The conglomerate and tufa are identical throughout, and it may be reasonably inferred, that the whole was once a long point, against which the waves of an ancient ocean acted, unparried by coral reefs. Near the summit of the outer island, about one hundred feet high, there is a neat circular well, fifteen feet deep and four feet in diameter, worn out of the solid tufaceous rock. Its sides are smooth and even, leaving no doubt that it was excavated by the action of water. This natural well is connected below with a horizontal chamber, which opens on the face of the rocky bluff. Another horizontal cavern near by extended several rods into the hill; but it was too low for exploration. The character of the caverns, and the nature of the place —at the head of a deep valley which opens on the sea—tell us of some former age when the ocean washed these shores. The place reminded us of the blow-holes which are still common among these Pacific islands. The horizontal caverns are slowly enlarging, by a kind of exfoliation usual in soft granular sedimentary rocks; the sand above peels off slowly, in consequence of the crystallization of common salt, or some of the saline minerals which are formed in caverns. This process raises the floor more than the increase in height: so that this enlarging process actually diminishes the passage. The walls of the well are firm, and are not undergoing this kind of enlargement.

Are coral islands growing from the depths of the oceans?

This question is in many minds, the prominent one connected with coral formations; and although abundantly answered in the preceding chapters, we give here, in concluding, a more formal reply. This reply is a simple negative; and a single fact establishes its truth. The reef-forming coral zoophytes, as has been shown, cannot grow at greater depths than 100 or 120 feet; and therefore in seas deeper than this, the formation or growth of reefs over the bottom is impossible.

Coral reefs instead of being a curse to the ocean and the adventurous mariner, have afforded the lofty islands a protection against the waves; they have gathered the debris of the abrading land-streams into shore flats, the seats of many of the villages and cocoanut groves of the islands; they have produced about these islands large numbers of safe harbors for shipping, with inland navigation for the native craft, besides dotting the waters around with green islets.

They have also studded the oceans with coral islands, as other lands have disappeared, and established many an excellent haven amid the waves. Like garlands they lie on the waters, but the "everlasting hills" are not more endúring.

ADDENDA.

P. 18. A calcareous crust of recent origin, in some cases occupies depressions in the exterior surface of the hills of coral sand-rock. These hills are of beach origin, and although 50 or 60 feet thick, consist throughout of the coral rock, having a sandy texture and generally laminated. There is nothing crust-like in their structure, any more than in the red sandstones of the Connecticut river. We are led to make this explanation by a wrong use made of the facts by a recent writer.

P. 57. The following are figures of other crystals of gypsum, which were crystallized from a drop of sea-water, under a microscope, while the author was examining some minute oceanic crustacea, in the Atlantic, latitude 11° S., longitude 12° West.

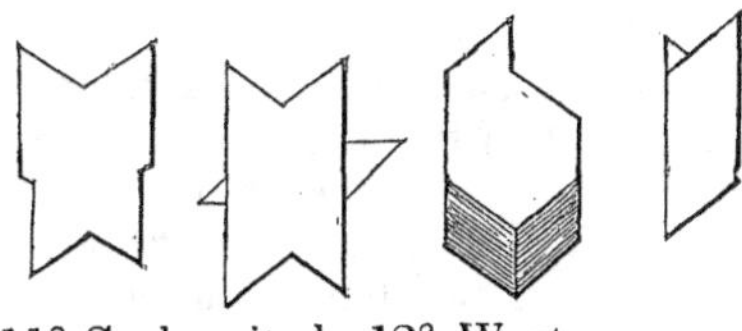

P. 58. The following is the mean of several recent analyses of the sea, in the Laboratory of L. Mulder (J. f. pr. Chem., lv, 499, 1852), together with analyses by Figuier and Mialhe, Regnault, and Riegel. The waters were those of the Atlantic or North Sea.

	L. Mulder.	F. & M.	Regnault.	Riegel.
Chlorid of Sodium, . .	78·5	78·9	76·5	75·2
" Magnesium, . .	9·4	8·6	10·2	9·0
Sulphate of Magnesia, . .	6·4	7·7	6·5	6·0
" Lime, . .	4·4	3·7	4·0	7·6
Chlorid of Potassium, . .	1·0	0·25	2·0	0·9
Bromid of Magnesium, . .	0·17	0·4	0·1	0·5
Carbonate of Lime, . .	0·04	0·4	0·1	0·5
Silica, ...	0·009	0·05		
Ammonia, ...	0·13			

P. 61, 97. The temperature 66° F., stated as limiting coral reef seas, is nearly, if not quite, the *extreme* temperature. The *mean of the coldest month* along the boundary is 68° F.

P. 106. The absence of coral from the coast of China is due to the temperature of the waters. The author has found, on further investigation, that on no part of the coast of China the sea has the temperature of 68° F. in winter. The winter line of 68° bends northward on approaching the coast of China, and includes the island of Loochoo; but it is then deflected abruptly to the south and terminates at latitude 15° N., on the coast of Cochin China.

On the African coast, there are coral reefs at Port Natal, in latitude 30° South; and here, owing to the warm currents from the Indian Ocean, the sea temperature is not below 68° F., any part of the year.

P. 115. The following citations from the Journal of C. Darwin, Esq., are important in their bearing on the subject of the consolidation of coral sands:

In his Journal, p. 588, he says:—"Lieutenant Evans informs me that during the six years he has resided on this Island (Ascension) he has always observed that in the months of October and November, when the sand [of a calcareous beach] commences travelling towards the southwest, the rocks which are situated at the end of the long beach become coated by a white, thick, and very hard calcareous layer. I saw portions of this remarkable deposit, which had been protected by an accumulation of sand. In the year 1831 it was much thicker than during any other period. It would appear that the water charged with calcareous matter, by the disturbance of a vast mass of calcareous particles only partially cemented together, deposits this substance on the first rocks against which it impinges. But the most singular circumstance is, that in the course of a couple of months, this layer is either abraded or redissolved, so that after that period, it entirely disappears. It is curious thus to trace the origin of a periodical incrustation, on certain isolated rocks, to the motion of the earth with relation to the sun; for this determines the atmospheric currents which give direction to the swell of the ocean, and this again the arrangement of the sea-beach, and this again the quantity of calcareous matter held in solution by the waters of the neighboring sea."

Mr. Darwin, speaking of a large beach of calcareous sand composed of comminuted and rounded fragments of shells and corals at Ascension, says, "The lower part of this, from the percolation of water containing calcareous matter in solution, soon becomes consolidated and is used as a building stone; but some of the layers are too hard for fracture, and when struck by the hammer, ring like flint."—Journal, p. 587.

See further on the subject of consolidation, a paper by Prof. Horsford in the American Journal of Science, [2], xiv, 245, and another by the author, ibid, xiv, 410.

INDEX.

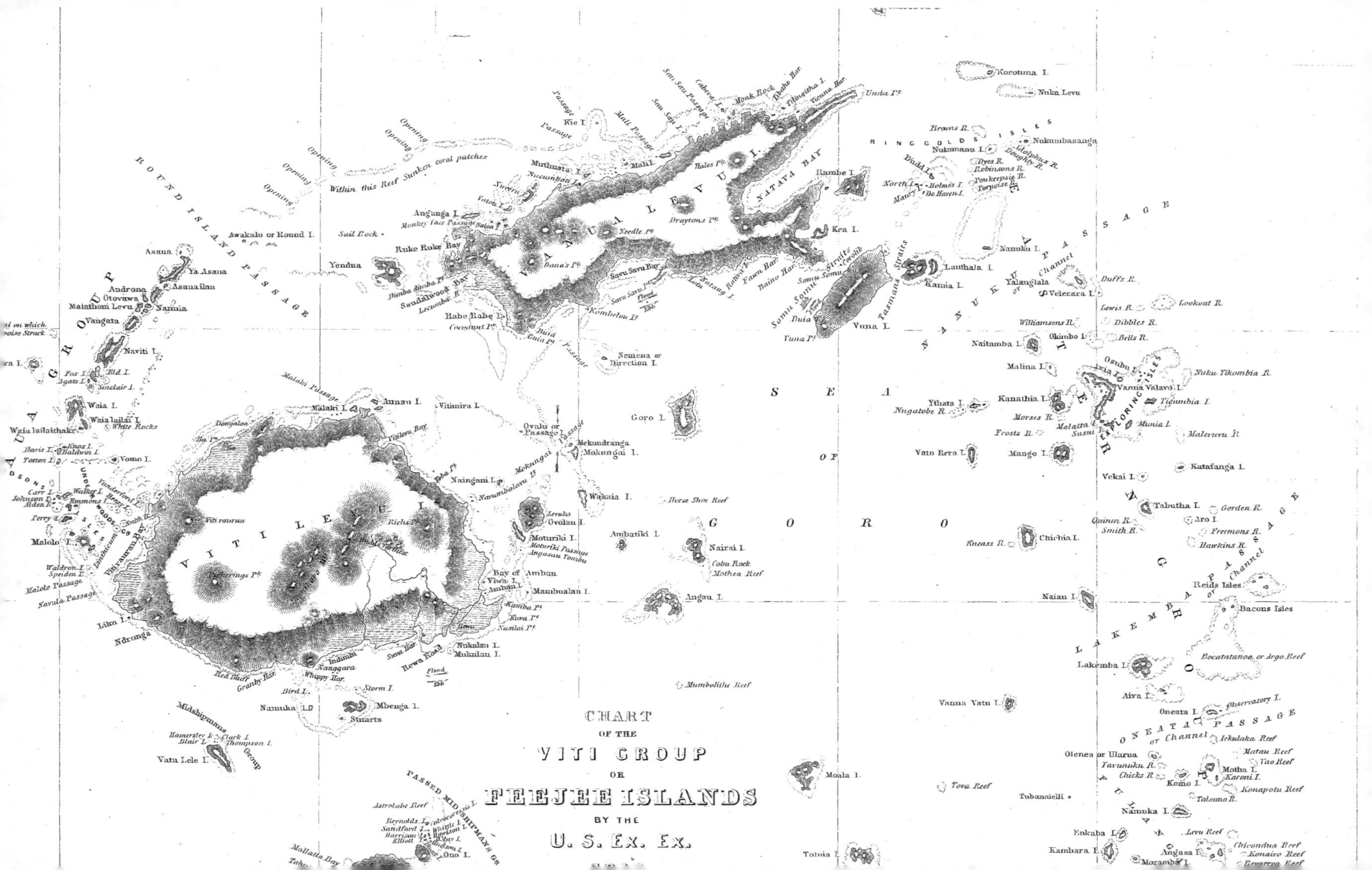

CHART
OF THE
VITI GROUP
OR
FEEJEE ISLANDS
BY THE
U. S. Ex. Ex.

ROUND ISLAND PASSAGE
Opening
Opening
Opening
Opening
Opening
Within this Reef Sunken coral patches
Awakalo or Round I.
Sail Rock
Asaua
Ya Asaua
Androna
Otovawa
Asauailau
Matathom Levu
Namuia
Vangata
ASAUA GROUP
Naviti I.
Fox I.
Bld I.
Sinclair I.
Waia I.
Waia lailai I.
Waia lailaithake
White Rocks
Davis I.
Knox I.
Baldwin I.
Totten I.
Vomo I.
UNDERWOODS GROUP
Carr I.
Walker I.
Johnson I.
Alden I.
Emmons I.
Vanderford I.
Henry I.
Perry I.
Smith I.
Malolo I.
Inndracum
Viti rauvau Bay
Waldron I.
Speiden I.
Malolo Passage
Navula Passage
Liku I.
Ndronga
VITI LEVU
Vitirauvau
Dickerings Pt.
Richs Pt.
Malaki Passage
Malaki I.
Aunau I.
Vitimira I.
Viti levu Bay
Naingani I.
Navambolavu Is.
Mokungai Passage
Ovalu or Passage
Mekundranga
Mokungai I.
Wakaia I.
Levuka
Ovolau I.
Moturiki I.
Moturiki Passage
Angasau Tombu
Bay of Amban
Viwa I.
Amban I.
Maunbualau I.
Kamba Pt.
Kuwa Pt.
Nasilai Pt.
Nukulau I.
Mukulau I.
Rewa Road
Flood
Ebb
Indimbi
Nanggara
Whippy Har.
Red Bluff
Granby Har.
Bird I.
Storm I.
Namuka I.
Mbenga I.
Stuarts
Midshipmans Group
Hamersley I.
Clark I.
Blair I.
Thompson I.
Vatu Lele I.
PASSED MIDSHIPMANS GR.
Astrolabe Reef
Reynolds I.
Sandford I.
Harrison I.
Elliott I.
Ono I.
Mallatta Bay
Totoia I.
Moala I.
Goro I.
Horse Shoe Reef
Ambatiki I.
Nairai I.
Cobu Rock
Mothea Reef
Angau I.
Mumbolithe Reef
SEA OF GORO
Yendua
Ruke Ruke Bay
Anganga I.
Monkey Face Passage
Dimba dimba Pt.
Sandalwood Bay
Lecumba R.
Rabe Rabe I.
Cocoanut Pt.
Buia Pt.
Passage
Kombelou Is.
Nemena or Direction I.
VANUA LEVU
Dana's Pt.
Needle Pt.
Draytons Pt.
Hales Pt.
Savu Savu Bay
Savu Savu Pt.
Natang I.
Rativa I.
Fawn Har.
Baino Har.
Somu Somu Straits
Buia
Tuna Pt.
Vuna I.
Tasmans Straits
NATAVA BAY
Kea I.
Rambe I.
Muthuata I.
Nucumbasi I.
Kie I.
Mali I.
Mali Passage
Sau Sau I.
Sau Sau Passage
Monk Rock
Rhathe Har.
Tilingitha I.
Vicuna Har.
Unda Pt.
Korotuna I.
Nuku Levu
RINGGOLDS ISLES
Browns R.
Nukumanu I.
Nukumbasanga
Adolphus R.
Doughty R.
Budd I.
Dyes R.
Robinsons R.
Poukeepsie R.
Porpoise R.
North I.
Holmes I.
Maury I.
De Haven I.
NANUKU PASSAGE
Namuka I.
Lauthala I.
Kamia I.
Yalanglala
Nanuku Channel
Velecara I.
Duffs R.
Lookout R.
Lewis R.
Dibbles R.
Williamsons R.
Okimbo I.
Bells R.
Naitamba I.
Malina I.
Osubu I.
EXPLORING ISLES
Nuku Tikombia R.
Vanua Valavo I.
Tieumbia I.
Munia I.
Malevuvu R.
Ythata I.
Nugatobe R.
Kanathia I.
Morses R.
Malatta
Susui I.
Frosts R.
Vatu Rera I.
Mango I.
Katafanga I.
Vekai I.
Tabutha I.
Gorden R.
Aro I.
Quinun R.
Smith R.
Fremons R.
Hawkins R.
Kneass R.
Chichia I.
LAKEMBA PASSAGE or Channel
Reids Isles
Bacons Isles
Naiau I.
Bocatatanoa or Argo Reef
Lakemba I.
Aiva I.
Vanna Vatu I.
Oneata I.
Observatory I.
ONEATA PASSAGE or Channel
Iekulaka Reef
Olenea or Ularua
Tarunuku R.
Matau Reef
Tao Reef
Chicks R.
Motha I.
Karoni I.
Komo I.
Konapotu Reef
Taloumo R.
Tova Reef
Tubanaielli
Namuka I.
Levu Reef
Enkaba I.
Kambara I.
Angasa I.
Moramba I.
Chicondua Reef
Konaivo Reef
Rewarewa Reef

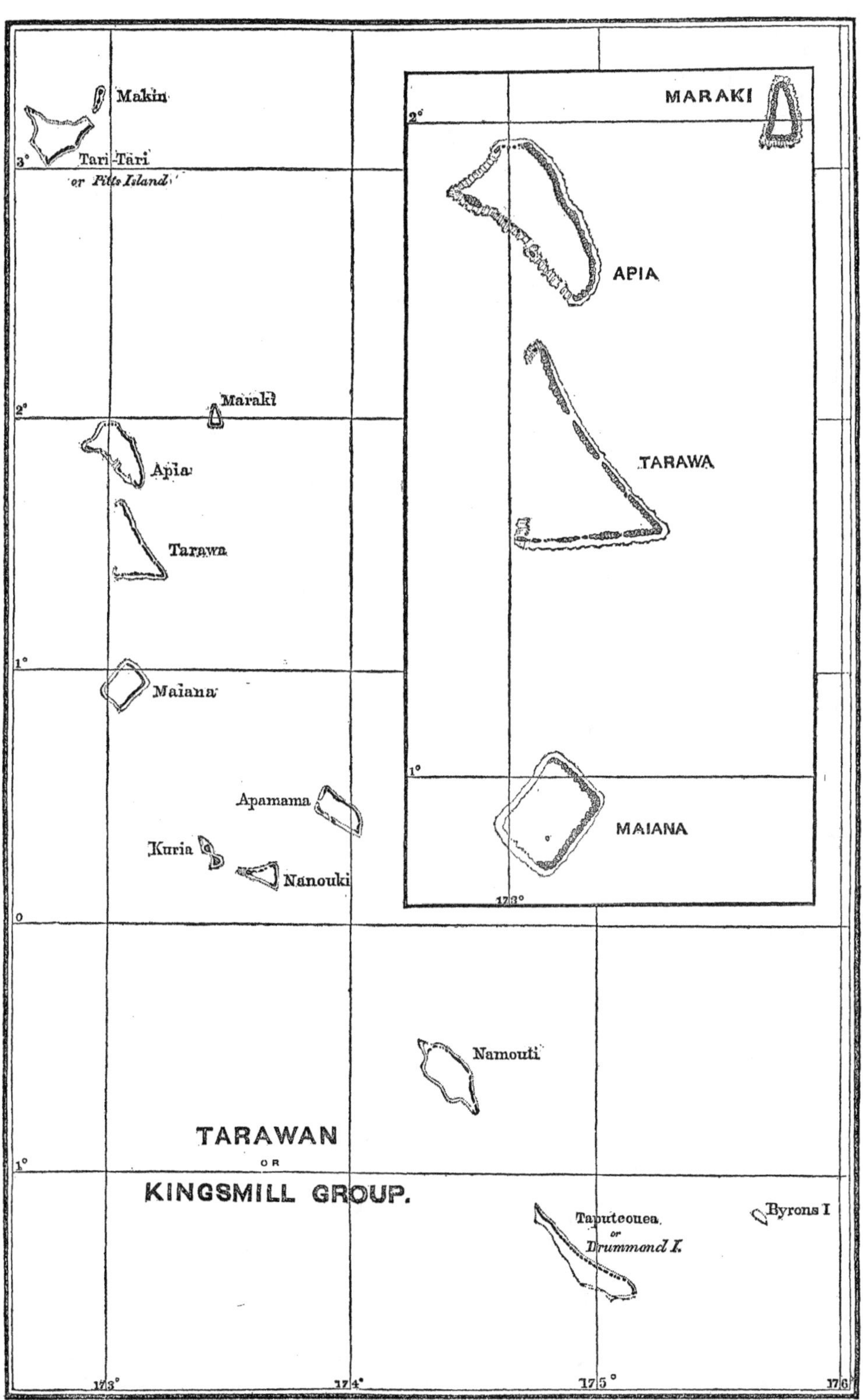
Makin
Tari-Tari
or Pitts Island
Maraki
Apia
Tarawa
Maiana
Apamama
Kuria
Nanouki
Namouti
TARAWAN
OR
KINGSMILL GROUP.
Taputeouea
or
Drummond I.
Byrons I
MARAKI
APIA
TARAWA
MAIANA
3°
2°
1°
0
1°
173°
174°
175°
176

www.ingramcontent.com/pod-product-compliance
Lightning Source LLC
LaVergne TN
LVHW021409110826
845150LV00007B/1848